INTERIOR DECORATING WITH PLANTS

Books by Carla Wallach

The Reluctant Weekend Gardener

Gardening in the City

Interior Decorating with Plants

INTERIOR DECORATING WITH PLANTS

Carla Wallach

COLLIER BOOKS *A DIVISION OF*
MACMILLAN PUBLISHING CO., INC.
NEW YORK

COLLIER MACMILLAN PUBLISHERS
LONDON

Macmillan Publishing Co., Inc.
866 Third Avenue, New York, N.Y. 10022
Collier Macmillan Canada, Ltd.

Library of Congress Cataloging in Publication Data

Wallach, Carla.
Interior decorating with plants.

Bibliography: p.
Includes index.
1. House plants in interior decoration.
I. Title.
SB419.W23 1976b 747'.9 76-15019
ISBN 0-02-012000-1

INTERIOR DECORATING WITH PLANTS is also published in a hardcover edition by Macmillan Publishing Co., Inc.

First Collier Books Edition 1976

Designed by Philip Grushkin

Printed in the United States of America

CONTENTS

ACKNOWLEDGMENTS

My deep appreciation to Dr. Pascal P. Pirone, Senior Plant Pathologist of The New York Botanical Garden, and Miss Elizabeth C. Hall, Senior Librarian, The Horticultural Society of New York and Associate Curator of Education Emeritus of The New York Botanical Garden, for their assistance in checking my notes.

This book could not have been as handsomely illustrated without the co operation of interior decorators. The gracious help received from these designers across the country has been invaluable. Special thanks go to interior designers Dick Ridge and Lafe Hill for their interest and helpful suggestions.

Although they are acknowledged elsewhere in the book, I want to thank those business firms and manufacturers for the information and photographs of their products. I also appreciate the help given by the *Architectural Digest* and *Interior Design* magazines and by the American Institute of Interior Designers (A.I.D.) and the National Society of Interior Designers (N.S.I.D.).

I am most grateful to Constance Schrader for her suggestions, patience, and unbounded enthusiasm. I am fortunate to have had her as my editor and friend.

And warmest thanks to my husband, Philip, for his encouragement.

INTRODUCTION

Research for this book included consulting interior decorators and horticulturists, taking down their views on the use of indoor plants in the home and in the office. It came as no surprise to discover that their respective philosophies often were diametrically opposite. Decorators and designers claim that plant growers are knowledgeable about the culture of plants but certainly not about how to show them off to best effect in the home—while ardent plant hobbyists most vehemently denounce designers as ignorant of horticultural practices, using plants only to give a touch of color to a room, blissfully unaware of what it takes to have plants survive indoors.

I agree and disagree with both sides. The beautiful and the functional *can* be united, perhaps not to the degree that each would like, but sufficiently so that each need not suffer at the expense of the other. I am only too aware that while the many superb interiors one sees gloriously pictured in home magazines show effective use of plants from a design point of view (as with throw pillows or fur rugs casually draped over a couch), they are disastrous insofar as the culture of the plants is involved. Saucers are nowhere in sight to catch the necessary drainage water, or else every plant is potted in a container without holes, which is worse! Geraniums are on a coffee table twenty feet from the nearest window. Shade-loving plants are in a brilliantly sunny alcove, or so dangerously close to the fireplace (if not indeed cascading from the mantle) that they would be cooked vegetables should the owner light the logs. We who grow plants because we dearly love them shudder every time we see such examples.

But let's look at the other side. Can't plants be placed where they properly belong, according to their needs, and still be displayed attractively? Can't we avail ourselves of the good taste and the knowledge of design and color that can be obtained from decorators? To a plant, a pot is a pot, a container a container; therefore, why not select the right one, not only for the health of the plant but also for the room and the "personality" of the plant? If plants can thrive and do double duty by hiding some ugly spot in a room, why not take advantage of it? We already know that they turn a pretty room into a spectacular one, but it takes the trained eye to know how to achieve this—when to use one "accent" plant or when to group several together. There are numerous plant stands, all functional, but one may fit in better with certain furnishings than another.

I have seen homes where plants flourish gloriously—in old, stained pots, resting in makeshift saucers or in undisguised aluminum pans. No attempt is made to reconcile the plants with the rest of the otherwise attractive room. I regret this as much as the previously mentioned decorators' masterpieces with horticulturally misplaced plants. This disdain of decor deprives the plant of its potential to look its best, much like a beautiful woman in an ill-fitting, cheap dress. Scattering pots here and there in a room does nothing either for the room or the plants, yet this is frequently seen in plant-loving homes.

Nature has given us so many plants to choose from, of different habits and needs, that I find it hard to believe we can't incorporate the healthy growth of plants into the beauty of our home furnishings. There is no reason why both sides cannot live happily together, and in this book I hope to act as a "broker" between the two highly creative and vocal (!) factions.

We all know that the ideal situation is where plants are grown in one part of the home and shown off in another. The grooming, nursing, "resting," are all done behind the scenes, and only those plants at their peak of beauty are brought forth for the delight of family and friends. Such luxury of space is available to relatively few. Spacious houses are rapidly disappearing. Unless designed specifically with plant-growing in mind, every square foot is spoken for in the average home. Apartment dwellers are perpetually short of space. Of course, gardening hobbyists will always find room—even if it's a bridge table smack in the middle of the living room. But people who want plants primarily to decorate the home must rely on a tiny makeshift corner somewhere for the basic "repair" work and on the actual "showcase" spot to do the rest. This is tough going, but here is where knowledge of the right plants for specific purposes is imperative. This spells the difference between success and failure. If a plant is happy where it's placed, it will give a minimum of trouble insofar as its health is concerned. During its so-so period (plants have ups and downs like people), it's an easy matter to screen it from view temporarily by placing other thriving plants strategically.

Plants have come a long way from the days when they were grown by little old ladies in sneakers, who were the pillars of garden clubs. As modern technology engulfs us more and more in its computer-programmed grip, we respond increasingly to an urge deep within ourselves to feel, touch, smell and see a living plant—not just once in a while, but as part of our own personal environment. The plant becomes an emissary of the once readily accessible but now often unattainable great outdoors. It is quite literally a breath of fresh air. A plant exacts just enough attention to remind us of its existence. As with a pet, one can't just buy it and then forget about it. It depends on us for its very life, and we should respond gratefully to being so needed.

As with everything else today, plants have risen in cost, giving us yet another good reason for choosing wisely at the neighborhood plant shop. While plants give far more in return than the original investment indicates, nevertheless one can spend a sizeable amount to create a lush indoor garden, and consequently, one hopes the plants will survive and continue to give us pleasure for a long time. It must be expected that some will not make it. Even the pros who grow them for a living expect to lose some. But if these basic conditions are met, one should enjoy long-lived, vigorous plants: 1) buying only healthy plants from a reputable dealer; 2) making sure of correct placement of the plant in the home, meeting its particular cultural needs; 3) observing sound horticultural practices (proper soil, watering, correct potting, etc.).

The book is divided into three major sections which follow one another with good reason. The first section stretches the imagination by showing us what others have done with plants. Most of us live in homes that fall short of perfection—beams stick out where they shouldn't, views from windows are less than inspiring, kitchens are cold-looking for all their functional splendor, and bathrooms can appear downright antiseptic, to list just a few examples. And even rooms that are dripping with super-chic elegance and perfection in every detail can gain something with the addition of plants.

The second part of the book translates the idea into reality, suggesting which plants are most suitable for the particular "job" you want done. If you've decided on hanging baskets for a north window—which plants should you buy? The last section discusses the selection of containers and the care of plants. There is no mystique about the cultivation of indoor plants, any more than that of plants outdoors—there are only sensible practices. A "green thumb" gardener is merely one who learns a few simple rules and follows them.

The illustrations in this book come from several sources. Friends and acquaintances graciously allowed me into their homes to photograph their highly personal gardening creations. These people long ago wedded their horticultural skills to their knowledge of good interior design, and the results are healthy, thriving plants, superbly at home in charming rooms.

Other photographs are primarily of interiors done by top designers. These also are rich in ideas of what plants can do for a room—whether living room, bedroom, bathroom, halls, etc. Some I deliberately chose even though I knew that there was something wrong horticulturally. This I point out under the photograph. But if the decorator's idea is truly topnotch, why not interpret it with suitable plants? It's the *effect* that counts in design. If trailing lantanas are shown cascading lavishly down a planter-divider, and we know they won't survive in that spot but shade-loving hanging begonias will, is the original idea worth any less for switching plant varieties? Indeed not.

The bibliography is for those who, hopefully, wish to learn a good deal more about plants and their fascinating world. Whether confined to a small room or expanding in the great outdoors, gardening is an immensely rewarding hobby.

Man designed the handsome decorative arts with which we surround ourselves today, and Nature created plants in all their splendor—let's merge the two and see what a beautiful world we really live in!

INDOOR GARDENS

PLANTS ARE HANDSOME—this we know. But do we fully utilize their ability to highlight a particularly handsome room, or to mask problems in a room of no special distinction? The uses of plants in the home are numerous, if we give them half a chance. There's a world of difference between growing house plants and cultivating indoor gardens. In the case of the former, plants are grown for the sake of growing plants. In the latter, plants are grown with a specific purpose in mind: to enhance the interior design of the home.

An indoor garden is planned; it doesn't just happen. It needn't be elaborate. A dozen geraniums on glass shelves in a sunny window can qualify as an indoor garden if care is taken to see that they are in spotless containers complementary to the room's furnishings. A garden can be a grouping of plants too, or a low and bushy divider between a large entrance area and the living room. Important gardens can be created with indoor pools and fountains, sculpture, abstract art, driftwood and hollow logs. There is no limit to the imagination once it gets started. Let's explore the marvelous world of plants, not only from the traditional horticultural point of view, but also from the interior design concept.

Plants as Room Dividers

Many rooms today are too small to take solid partitions. Furniture and screens take away the open feeling that is so desirable. Plants, however, can create the *illusion* of partitioning. The need may be to create dining

space in a living room, or an entrance where none now exists; carving out a part of the bedroom for a sewing center, or for a hobby corner in a large dining room; or isolating a home office in the living room for the free-lance worker. Space is so precious today that home dwellers have to utilize every square inch, frequently making one room do the work of two.

There are many ways that plants can be used as room dividers. The variety of foliage makes them versatile tools. A popular idea is placing a couch at a right angle to the wall, backed by a long, narrow table (or planter) of the same height holding a collection of plants. The height and types of plants depend on how tall a partition is needed, and on the proportions and style of the room.

Etageres also divide a room without fencing it in. Again, the height of the etagere depends on the dimensions of the room. Plants on the shelves instead of the usual bric-a-brac contribute a calming, soothing influence to a room that may already be "busy" with accessories. Choose both upright and hanging plants, making sure that *both* sides of the etagere look attractive. Double-pot the plants to insure against any possible damage from overwatering.

Double-potting is mentioned many times in this book for good reason: it combines sound horticultural practices with good looks, by placing the pot in which the plant is grown (with drainage hole) inside a slightly larger, waterproof, attractive pot—called a cache-pot or jardiniere. Potting directly into the outside pot invites trouble since it is waterproof and would therefore prevent proper drainage. You might water just a bit too much and rot the roots of the plants. It's safer and more convenient to double-pot. Should the plant die or need reviving, it's a simple matter to replace it with another one. But even with double-potting, care must be taken that excess water does not collect at the bottom. This can be avoided by resting the inner pot on a layer of pebbles. Fill the space between the two pots with a mulch, covering the surface with it as well. Depending on the size of the pots, large or pea-sized gravel is good, as are marble chips, Perlite or moss. The type of mulching is the "finishing touch" to the art of double-potting, for it gives the appearance that the plant is growing directly in the outside container, totally hiding the pot in which the plant is growing. There's a practical side effect to mulching with moss, when the inner pot is made of clay—especially when you are going away on brief vacations. Water the plant thoroughly, moistening the mulch

An indoor garden can be as simple as this grouping of plants in a corner, or as elaborate as the atrium in the Walmsley residence pictured in the color insert. (*Photograph courtesy of Window Shade Manufacturers Association*)

as well. The porous clay will absorb the needed moisture and keep plant happy.

A striking room divider can be built around a piece of sculpture "anchored" with plants. A free-standing design, whether abstract or traditional, is not likely to have that "grotto" look. Plants should not compete with the sculpture if the latter is to be the focal point. The plants are added to create the divider.

The contemporary open-area concept, where one living area flows into another one without benefit of walls, presents one problem: the free-standing column which encloses a support beam. After all, beams are still needed to hold up the ceiling! Some people may not be bothered by their presence. Others object to them and look for ways to distract the eye from them. Since they are frequently located where a wall might normally exist, thereby dividing one area from another, a planter-divider can be incorporated around the column or post. A low, free-form floor planter encircling the column—perhaps even connecting the column with a wall—makes a dramatic indoor garden. Adequate light obviously must be provided, necessary with any indoor garden. Fortunately, today's modern apartment buildings and contemporary houses have vast areas of glass—entire walls or multiple windows—which allow a maximum amount of light.

If plants are tall enough, they can stand by themselves as room dividers. Group several bushy shrubs and trees zig-zag fashion to screen one area from another. Containers with hidden casters facilitate cleaning of rug or floor, but they're not easy to find. Wood stands with casters attached can be made by a carpenter and placed under the containers. They should be low and slightly smaller than the container, so no one will notice them. Clear, plastic stands are also available.

When selecting plant material to be used alone as a divider, let your eye be the judge as to type of foliage. Contrast is good, within reason. Extremely dainty, lacy leaves do not have much of an effect when placed next to thick, heavy foliage. Grouping several of the same type of plants together gives the best results if one wants a massive, important look. Variety and scale can be introduced by adding a few lower plants of a different kind entirely.

The very first impression of a home is made by the entrance hall. If there is ample light coming in from a nearby window (as in this picture) or from glass panels flanking the door, low-light plants can be used effectively. Otherwise, light fixtures have to be installed. (*Rex Reed residence by designer Dick Ridge*)

OPPOSITE, ABOVE: Ingredients needed for double-potting: plant, waterproof container, gravel, coarse moss and decorative green sheet moss. OPPOSITE, BELOW: Plant appears to be growing directly from the ornamental container. Actually, gravel is at the bottom, coarse moss fills the space between inner and outer pots, and green moss is on top, hiding everything neatly. The plant is not only handsomely displayed, but is kept cool and moist longer as a result of the moss mulch. (*Photograph by Brian Manning*)

BELOW: This is a striking example of plants as room dividers. The dining room in this contemporary home is divided from the rest of the house by a wide stone planter filled with trailing begonias. The dining room is several steps lower than the rest of the house, so that the begonias cascade magnificently down the dining-room side of the planter. For another view of this handsome room, see the photograph of the Schaffer residence in the color insert. (*Residence of Mr. and Mrs. Franklin Schaffer, Greenwich, Connecticut; photograph by Brian Manning*)

Plants are an airy extension of the free-standing fireplace, and together act as a divider between the living room and hallway. (*Designed by Joseph V. Freitag, A.I.D.; photograph by Ernie Silva*)

A limited budget is good reason for letting a far-out imagination go to town! Why not transform a coat rack into a fun room divider? Buy the same model that is rented from caterers, which holds about twenty-five coats. Paint it a flat black or moss green. Suspend a mass of baskets from the top rod, on chains of varying lengths which won't be seen because the plants cascade in uneven layers. The total effect is that of a wall of plants. Only lush, mature plants should be used, looking every bit as full viewed from one side as from the other. On the floor under the baskets, place plants on wicker trays which have waterproof liners containing one inch of pebbles. (Metal roasting pans or Pyrex baking pans are great as liners.) This floor arrangement has a double purpose: the plants on the floor meet the hanging baskets, thereby closing the gap of the "wall," and the trays catch any water dripping from the baskets. Of course, if the budget permits it, there's nothing against applying this same idea to a smashing antique rack! There are some fabulous one-of-a-kinds in brass or wrought iron.

Window Treatments

Our rapidly expanding population necessitating ever-increasing housing creates many problems—one being the loss of once-beautiful vistas of rolling countryside or of a fabulous skyline. Today, more often than not, we look out into someone else's backyard or apartment. When such is the case, plants offer an attractive way of screening out undesirable views. Hang baskets zig-zag style across the window, from chains fastened to the ceiling or to a heavy curtain rod. (See the hanging basket in the color photographic insert.) Since the purpose is to screen the outside view, large baskets are best—two lush, cascading baskets will cover a greater window area than will several small ones. While plants must have space for good air circulation, a profusion of greenery is the objective.

Another idea is to put glass shelves across the window to hold numerous small plants, choosing both upright and hanging varieties for contrast. All

ABOVE: A wall of windows can be used for an indoor garden with the installation of glass shelves holding many plants. The bold design of the room's furnishings demands this large-scale display of plants. (*Photograph courtesy of House Beautiful, copyright 1973, the Hearst Corporation*)

OPPOSITE: The simplest way of screening an unpleasant view and having a delightful garden at the same time is to put glass shelves across a window which can hold many plants. Note that all pots are similar, creating a unified design. If desired, trailing plants can be mixed with the others, further blocking outside view. (*Photograph by Gottscho-Schleisner*)

containers should match to avoid a cluttered look and focus attention on the plants. Either double-pot or have matching saucers (that holds true for *every* arrangement). One spectacular tree, or a grouping of several smaller ones, in front of a window will also distract the eye away from what's outside. Whatever camouflage trick is used, the principle is the same: by directing the eye to the plants rather than to the window, unattractive views can be cleverly masked, without shutting out the sunlight.

That old standby, the window sill, shouldn't be overlooked simply because there's a radiator underneath. If the sill isn't deep enough, extend it with a

shelf which is held by brackets or self-attached. Put a sheet of fiberglass (asbestos is frowned upon for environmental reasons) on top of the shelf, and place on that a waterproof tray half filled with pebbles that you keep moist all the time. Select tall plants—obviously to screen as large an area as possible. This idea can be combined very successfully with hanging baskets for really thorough coverage.

How to Cope with Large Glass Areas

Sometimes, too much of a good thing can present a problem. How fortunate if you have a bay window, a glass-enclosed porch or sun room, or enormous glass walls. Your home will always have a cheerful spot where you and your friends can gather in a relaxed mood. However, these glass areas can look cold and severe when left bare. They need plants to soften them, to accentuate the feeling of being outdoors. Lack of adequate light is not likely to be a problem, so take full advantage of it and go native!

A *bay window* (or an alcove, which can be synonymous) is a dramatic setting for an indoor garden. There are numerous possibilities to consider, one or all of which can be adopted, depending on the size of the window: glass shelves across the window areas to hold small plants, hanging baskets from the ceiling, a built-in or homemade planter following the curve of windows, plant stands, plants on the floor. It should be noted that each of these is a different distance from the window glass, thereby making possible the cultivation of several kinds of plants, from the extremely sun-demanding ones by the glass to the shade-loving ones on the floor below the planters.

The plants on the glass shelves are closest to the light, permitting flowering

Whether custom-built or homemade, planters for window areas afford the best way to display plants. Two levels make it possible to show off more plants, keeping the sun-loving ones near the window and those requiring more shade on the lower level. On top, pots are sunk in moss; below, they are standing on a bed of gravel. (*Photograph by Gottscho-Schleisner*)

plants or cacti. Stick to one kind of pot, although not necessarily the same size, for a neat and uncluttered look (with matching saucers, naturally). If the window faces south and if the summer sun in your area reaches scorching intensity, it may be necessary to have a thin screen between the shelves and the window glass to prevent the plants from getting burned. There is now a totally sheer window shade made of vinyl-coated fiberglass, called "comfort shade" (Joanna Western Mills Co.), which reduces solar heat penetration yet maintains see-through visibility and constant air flow. Sheer glass curtains also cut down excessive sunlight.

A built-in planter should be constructed, if at all feasible, following the contour of the bay window. Unless you are handy with tools, get a carpenter to build it, below the level of the window sill. Make sure sturdy support is provided to hold the weight of the plants. Fit the planter with a waterproof liner at least two inches high (sheet metal shops make galvanized metal liners to measure, painted with asphalt to retard rusting). Fill the liner halfway with pebbles kept moist, and place plants on top (no need to worry about saucers here). Be sure that the water level which keeps the pebbles moist remains below the surface—plant roots rot when in water for any length of time. Deeper planters are good for super-thirsty plants because pots can be sunk halfway up to their rims in a damp mixture of peat moss and vermiculite (instead of pebbles). Clay pots are imperative in this case, since the porous clay allows the moisture to seep through the pot right into the roots of the plant. If ornamental pebbles are used, cost can be kept down by filling the planter with coarse gravel and finishing off with a layer of attractive pea-sized gravel, marble chips or decorative stones.

Redwood is the preferred material for planters because of its long life and disregard of water dripping on it, humidity, heat, and so forth. It can be painted or stained to suit the decor of the room. Other usable materials are pine, cypress, cedar, plywood and other kinds of wood which also can be painted, stained, or covered with adhesive-backed materials which duplicate wood finishes. Obviously, one's budget determines how elaborate the planter is to be, but insofar as the functional is concerned, all one needs is a sturdy wooden box on legs, with a waterproof liner.

For those who rent their houses or apartments and don't like the expense of built-to-order planters, a similar effect can be achieved with several narrow tables or benches placed against the window sills, holding waterproof trays

A planter can take many forms, such as this extra-long, narrow table. A collection of ferns is a perfect foil for a cheery pot of daffodils in spring. (*Photograph by Gottscho-Schleisner*)

filled with pebbles. (Shallow metal or glass roasting pans are great for this.) Hide the pans in wicker trays spray-painted white or moss green.

Whether built-to-order or homemade, the above planters follow the lines of the bay window, leaving an open area in front and below which can be filled with still more plants, if one wishes, depending on the overall size of the bay window. Ready-made metal or wicker planters on legs can be bought to fill in this open space. Or a homemade planter can be constructed along the lines of a wide wooden stepladder, painted white or, better still, moss green, so that only the plants dominate. Whichever type of planter is used, it should be lower than the planter along the window sills. This creates a tiered design, allowing each level of plants to be seen. Mix hanging plants with upright ones so that legs of planters are hidden and the lovely look of cascading greenery is exploited.

Under the rear planter and at the base of the front planter, group shade-loving foliage plants. Ferns give a cool woodland look. Sheltered from direct light by the planters, these and other plants will thrive. Either double-potting or matching pots and saucers are necessary here.

Hanging baskets should not be overlooked in a bay window garden. Why waste the space above the planters? Hang a few baskets at different heights, a foot or so away from the windows so that the plants on the glass shelves can be seen easily. Hanging baskets should be made waterproof either through use of a deep saucer placed under the pot (both inside a rope hanger) or through double-potting.

In any large indoor garden, such as the bay window, selection of plant material is obviously dictated by your own personal preferences, and by the light and heat available. But whatever the plants chosen, group them with an eye to color and design. White flowers have a cooling effect and separate neighboring colors. Some plants are fragile-looking, with delicate foliage and dainty flowers—don't hide them behind plants with bold growing habits. When plants are part of a group, think of them in terms of the entire design, not only as individuals. This means applying the principles of landscape design inside the home, and why not? In an outdoor flower bed, given the proper soil and cultural requirements, annuals and perennials can be planted either without thought and prior plan, or with a very definite objective in mind. An

This planter is nothing more than a long shelf connected to the walls with support in the middle, yet it effectively shows off a collection of African violets. A few trailing plants near the edge would hide the wall beneath. (*Photograph by Gottscho-Schleisner*)

indoor garden can also demand planning and judgment. You provide the setting and the plants that are compatible with it. Next, you group the plants in such a way that they will be shown off at their prettiest, both for their benefit and for the decor of the room.

The advantage of a fairly large indoor garden is that it affords the opportunity of revolving plants that are dormant, placing them temporarily in an out-of-sight spot until they can once more stand in the limelight. This is important, especially if one has no working area where plants can be nursed back to vigorous health. Where only a few plants are grouped together, those in need of help are quickly seen. But in a large grouping, the sickly plants have a chance to recover in privacy. The eye is too busy admiring those that are at their peak.

If for no other reason than the health of your plants, cooperate with the energy crisis by shutting off any radiators in the bay window. Rely on the heat in the rest of the room to make this area comfortable. If this is impossible, create a buffer between the blast of hot air and the plants. Cover the window sill with a sheet of fiberglass and a wooden shelf to protect plants on shelves directly above. If heat comes through grills on the wall below the window sill, tack plywood to the backs of planters to prevent hot air from blowing on the plants. Check frequently to see that pebbles in trays are moist to offset excessive dryness of the air. Floor plants should also be set on saucers half filled with moist pebbles. The idea is to increase the humidity as much as possible.

A *glass-enclosed porch* can be almost as rewarding as a greenhouse, but there may be unreliability of temperature. The average heated sunporch has temperatures ranging from coldest near the glass walls or windows to warmest near the radiator grills. If electric heaters are used, there will also be pockets of warm and cool air. However, with a little flexibility and moving of plants until they find their right places, this can be overcome. Furnished with wicker or wrought iron furniture, this romantic pastoral room is a natural setting for masses of hanging baskets, planters on the floor or plants on glass-topped tables. If winters are severe, it's best to keep plants away from the glass areas. Be sure to know how low the temperature dips during the night. The best range is 55 to 65 degrees, and the high 40's is just about as low as you should get. Don't select plants that are native to the tropics for this room, unless you are certain that your night temperature stays above 55 degrees. Remember that during the day, the sun can make the room's temperature zoom way into the high 80's or more. Not all plants will welcome this yo-yo environment, so buy one plant at a time and see what happens. If it thrives, stick with it.

If you've always wanted an indoor pool, a sunporch is the ideal place to fulfill this desire. First ask yourself if you want to listen to water trickling all the time. It can drive some people right up the wall. But if you like it, install a small fountain and group plants around the rim. Forget water plants inside the fountain because plants don't relish water dripping over their heads. However, if you forgo moving water, a water garden is far simpler to achieve than it looks. Have the pool at least 10 inches deep so you can sink pots of plants right up to their rims. Put two to three inches of sandy soil mixture at the bottom of the pool. There's really no need for a fancy drainage system. Use a garden hose to siphon the water out sometimes, but this needn't be done frequently. The main idea is to simulate a tiny woodland pool, and those are always dark and murky-looking. I have in mind my pond in Connecticut, which, because of its humus bottom, is so black that it reflects the sky, clouds and surrounding trees and plants as if it were a flawless mirror. It's quite beautiful and natural because nature made it. To create such an effect, edge your small indoor pool with rocks (if the real thing is impossible to get, substitute Featherock, artificial but amazingly real-looking). Copy nature further and insert moss between the rocks (a few packages of green sheet moss should do the trick).

For plants outside the pool, select ferns to give the garden an authentic look. Add several kinds of rex begonias for color, and a few pots of ivy to soften the outlines of the rocks. For inside the pool, water lilies are an obvious choice. Since there is no worry about freezing, you can indulge in exotic tropical lilies (as opposed to hardy lilies, which come in all colors except blue and have no fragrance). Plant the lilies in pots submerged to the rims. Shops specializing in aquariums sell all kinds of water plants, such as *Myriophyllum, Anacharis, Salvania, Azolla* and others. The size of pool dictates how many plants you'll need, but don't overdo the vegetation. You want to see the water.

To keep the water clean and maintain the proper ecological balance, include a few goldfish and snails. Fish breathe oxygen in and carbon dioxide out, and plants do the reverse; you can appreciate how wonderfully nature works to have all her creations complement one another so efficiently. Good light is essential to the success of a water garden, which is why the heated porch is a fine location. A water temperature of 60 degrees or more is necessary for both plants and fish.

A natural water garden is not the place for decorative cache-pots. Clay pots or wooden tubs are most appropriate for plants surrounding a pool. Well-weathered logs hollowed out to hold small pots of ferns make a charming background for a woodland pool. Keep trying all sorts of designs until your eye is entirely satisfied that the water garden looks as if it had been transplanted from the woods. If you are fortunate enough to have a greenhouse which adjoins the house, and if it has a corner for sitting and relaxing, you might consider putting a water garden there. It would be the first thing I would do! Unfortunately, my greenhouse is free-standing, away from the house, and strictly a "working" greenhouse.

Glass walls used to be a joke. You paid the builder extra money to have a dramatic wall of solid glass, and you ended up looking into the neighbor's living room through *his* glass wall! It's no longer amusing because one sees so many of these suburban victims of the last decade's housing boom. Rather than resort to drawn draperies twenty-four hours a day, why not turn this glass area into an indoor garden? Plants will take the eye away from the view outside (as in the case of windows with undesirable views).

A built-to-order floor planter is one solution. One side is made flush with the wall while the rest is free form, which is more graceful than if it were a severe rectangle. If possible, it should be deep enough to submerge the largest pot. One sees so many elaborate planters with pots of all sizes showing above the surface—a few more inches in depth, and the design would have been far more attractive. The object of a planter in the first place is to hide pots, uniting the plants and making them look as if they were growing right there. Otherwise, the plants could just as well be grouped right on the floor, without benefit of planter. In fact, this is the best way to start planning a floor planter: group all plants in front of the glass wall and move them about until you have the desired effect. With a length of rope or a hose, outline the area the plants are to cover. That will be the outline for the free-form planter. At the same time, measure the height of the tallest pot. That, plus a few more inches, will be the depth of the planter. Obviously, use judgment. If you have a pot more than one foot deep, consider having some of it show above mulch if you want a shallow planter.

A carpenter can build the planter out of any wood or wood finish you desire to fit in with the room's decoration. Remember that it can be stained or painted anything you want, but the simpler the better. A dark wood finish is my preference, as it doesn't distract from the plants. Fitted inside, also built to order, must be a waterproof, galvanized metal liner made by a sheet metal shop. This combination of planter-liner is the best permanent installation you can have—other than a stone planter. In a pinch, a double layer of thick plastic will do, but if you're going to have a planter made to order, you might as well have the permanent liner made as well and get a good job done.

Plants soften the starkness of glass walls. When the outside view is desirable, keep plants low except in the corner where walls meet. If neighboring construction needs blocking out, tall foliage plants make a good screen. (*Photograph by Gottscho-Schleisner*)

But what about the apartment dweller who has a glass wall with a similar unattractive view, but who doesn't wish to go to the expense of building in something which he won't be able to use in his next home? A little expertise in the fine art of camouflage will see you through. First cover the area to be "planted" with heavy plastic. Next, let your ingenuity work to improvise a planter. Anything which is waterproof suits the purpose, so long as it is several inches deep. Try a triple row of ordinary roasting pans (either metal or glass), or plastic laundry baskets. Place this "planter" on the plastic sheet, along the glass wall. Fill it with gravel.

Next comes the "edging." It should be at least half an inch higher than the planter. It can be bricks, concrete blocks, cork, plywood or molding; look around at your neighborhood lumber yard and you'll get lots of ideas. As long as the edging hides the planter and looks attractive, it suits the purpose. Either set the pots on the gravel or sink them to their rims, depending on the depth of the planter and the size of the pots. Fill the gap between planter and edging with more pebbles, so that everything is hidden and only a clean sweep of mulch shows. Do the same with spaces between each "planter." If, for example, six roasting pans are used to make the planter, together with a brick edging, cover the entire area with pebbles (or some other mulch) so that only the bricks show as a clean edge to the entire planter. By bringing the plastic lining right up against the inside of the bricks, pebbles won't escape through whatever tiny cracks there might be between the bricks.

Have plants in matching, spotless, clay pots. If you do sink them, hide them completely under the pebbles. Plants will appear to be growing right out of the mulch, creating the desired effect of a unified indoor garden.

Instead of small pebbles, a mixture of small and large stone is suitable as a mulch. Nothing too large should be used by itself because it cannot camouflage as easily. Pebbles or shredded bark slip easily into tiny cracks; so does Perlite, which is best used with cacti and succulents because these require little water. It has been my experience that Perlite dries quickly. Vermiculite remains moist for a long time and is good to use with thirsty plants; it's not all that pretty, so it should get a top dressing of pebbles or shredded bark.

In selecting plants for a glass-wall planter, keep variety as well as contrast in mind. The size of the planter determines how much variety you can have. As with a flower bed outdoors, it's better to have several plants of two varieties than to have eight different kinds of plants. The latter is a hodge-podge of plants resembling a nursery or a city plant shop display. Have one tall, dramatic tree, to admire against the glass wall in silhouette during the day, and against whatever covering material is used at night. Add two or three shrubs with good-looking foliage, and put ferns and begonias at the base. A thick grouping of ivy pots can form an attractive ground cover. If there's plenty of sun during the day, try flowering plants for color. If the planter is shallow, remember that strategically placed low plants hide the pots of larger plants. If the view outside the glass wall is really a disaster, concentrate on tall, bushy plants with lush foliage.

Hide That Air Conditioner!

Many people have an individual room air conditioner, but deplore its appearance. Designers have many clever ideas for hiding it without blocking the flow of cool air, but these are usually built-to-order designs. There's a less costly way to camouflage it and gain an indoor garden in the bargain.

The first step is to paint the panels which extend from the sides of the appliance to the window wall the same color as the walls of the room. This avoids the "breaking up" of space. Next, determine the direction of air flow. Turn the fan to its highest speed and aim air flow straight up, or out into the room if no one is going to be seated nearby. The latter is the better choice because it allows you to have plants above as well as to the sides of the air conditioner.

Hang baskets from brackets on either side, and from chains hooked into the window ceiling. Add plants on the window sill at either side of the appliance, if space permits, and you have a jungle encircling the air conditioner! Unless vents are located on top of the appliance, place a waterproof tray there, and set plants in it on a layer of pebbles. During the winter months when the appliance is not used, choose large pots of hanging plants which cascade down the front. It's mighty hard to detect what's behind this jungle of green, and the entire window is a beautiful garden to behold.

If the air flow must go upwards, anything hanging overhead must be omitted during summer months. Rely on baskets and plants at either side of the air conditioner to soften its looks. Choose mature plants of bushy habit, such as grape ivy, asparagus fern, spider plant or ruffled ivy, for best coverage.

Murals Need Plants

A *trompe l'oeil* effect is the reason one chooses a mural or scenic wallpaper for a wall. The object is to fool the eye by drawing it into another world: a summer garden, a Cape Cod beach, a Mediterranean landscape, a

ABOVE: Superb antique panels are the focal point of this magnificent room. The tall, delicate plant is just the right accent for the space between panels and cabinet. (*Apartment of designer Dick Ridge; photograph by Brian Manning*)

OPPOSITE: The dinette area in the author's apartment kitchen has a wallpaper mural which adjoins cabinets. An abrupt break in the optical illusion is avoided by placing a plant between the wall cabinets and the mural. (*Photograph by Brian Manning*)

tropical shore, etc. This open feeling enlarges a tiny room which might otherwise be dismally claustrophobic.

A small kitchen-dining area is a popular spot for the use of a mural, but the realistic effect is sometimes jarred when you see swaying palm trees melting into the hanging copper pans! Something is needed to create a "buffer zone." Plants can soften the transition from fantasy to reality, as well as contribute to the *trompe l'oeil* effect. Think of ferns with a woodland scene; palms with the tropics; a *Dracaena marginata* or a bamboo palm with an oriental motif. A "standard" tree on each side of a formal English garden mural can be especially handsome in a traditional dining room.

Keep in mind, however, that the objective is to soften the dividing line between wallpaper and whatever adjoins it, so choose plants that will be tall enough to do the job. They can stand on the floor or on a small table or counter. Usually there is a dado below the mural (a molding strip several feet from the floor which "frames" the bottom of the mural) so that there is no need in a tiny kitchenette to take up precious space with plants on the floor. Start at the dado line and measure from there.

Rx for Antiseptic Kitchens, Austere Bathrooms: Plants

You are not alone if you feel sometimes you should don cap, mask and sterilized gown when you enter the kitchen. While the current trend of design is away from the stark look, many of us have inherited such kitchens and bathrooms from previous owners. Plants do wonders for stainless steel, formica and cold porcelain. They bring a touch of warmth, cheer, sometimes whimsy if your mood dictates. Kitchens and baths are areas where you can have some fun and let your imagination go. What would be too "cute" or unsuitable in other rooms might be just right for a kitchen, such as a terra cotta animal filled with different herbs.

If your kitchen gets lots of sun, go in for flowering plants. Glass shelves on the window are the perfect place to grow herbs, wax begonias, geraniums and such. Keep trying different plants until you see which ones "take" to that spot. Have a "lazy susan" on the kitchen table and load it with small plants, or place a row of flowering pots along a sleek counter top. Hang plants from the ceiling or from wrought-iron racks made to hold pots and pans. Suspended from the ceiling, these racks hold a number of small baskets. Always hang baskets at different heights, not for better visibility, but for a more natural look.

Even the handsomest of kitchens can use plants as the finishing touch. Note the uniform white pots which blend with the tiles and don't distract from the plants. (*Photograph courtesy of House Beautiful, copyright 1973, the Hearst Corporation*)

A kitchen is full of items that lend themselves beautifully as containers. Consider a bread basket with small pots of herbs (line the basket with foil first); six small fluted soufflé dishes holding African violets; salad bowls, either wooden or amber or tortoiseshell plastic; pottery dishes filled with pebbles as containers for pots of cacti and succulents; earthenware platters as trays for small begonias; folding salad baskets used to dry salad greens serving as hanging planters (just place the pot and a saucer inside one and tie the handles to any chain or hook—great for all varieties of ivies). Just look around your kitchen and use your imagination. Take a stroll through the store that has a good housewares department. You'll get dozens of ideas on how to cheer up your kitchen.

For maximum effect, double-pot some of your plants in these "fun" containers and also have others in clay pots with matching saucers. Which you

These plants are in the dining area of a kitchen, but so lush and effective is the grouping that it could be in any room of the house. The more plants are grouped together, the greater the impact on the room; plants scattered here and there reduce the effect. The rough-surfaced wood planter goes well with the brick floor design. (*Photograph courtesy of the Flintkote Company*)

A spacious bathroom which features twin skylight planting areas was designed with plants in mind. Lighting and humidity are perfect for lush growth. (*Photograph courtesy of California Redwood Association*)

Whether old-fashioned bathrooms are streamlined or simply given a fresh new look, a warm touch can be added with a plant or two. This needn't be elaborate to be effective, as these two bathrooms prove. (*Photographs courtesy of Window Shade Manufacturers Association*)

use where depends on the arrangement of plants. Whenever you display plants in a row, as on shelves or on a counter, use only clay pots and saucers. If you wish to group half a dozen plants on a table, place them inside a container or on a tray. Always have a layer of pebbles at the bottom so that plants can draw needed moisture and humidity. Keep pebbles moist but not flooded.

Bathrooms are higher in humidity than other rooms in the home and therefore are choice locations for plants. As mentioned earlier, some bathrooms can verge on the antiseptic-looking, and can profit greatly by the addition of greenery. For that matter, the opposite is also true. A bathroom which is a riot of colors with boldly patterned linens can be "calmed down" by cool, green plants.

Show plants on shelves, hang them from the ceiling or put them on the floor, but use them lavishly! Wicker baskets sprayed white or a coordinating color are perfect to hold pots—remember to insert a waterproof tray or aluminum foil as a liner. As with clay, wicker adds warmth to any setting with its informal look. If your bathroom does double duty as a laundry room with washing machine and dryer, you need plants to take the eye away from these appliances. Use a large wicker tray to hold plants together with the usual bath oils and soaps, and so forth. It's easy to lift the tray with everything on it when you want to use the washer, if the latter is a top-loading style.

As with the kitchen, the bathroom is a place where you can drop your inhibitions and turn all sorts of plastic containers into planters. Train your eye to see uses for houseware items other than those for which they were originally intended. A wastebasket holds a tall plant; a Lucite tray is a large saucer for several pots; a small stepladder sprayed a bright color makes a great stand for numerous plants; a tall wicker stool is a pedestal for a mature, cascading Boston fern. Bamboo suitcases or trunks make handsome planters when sprayed a bright color or left natural (I'm partial to flat white or pale moss green). Drill holes in the cover and drop pots up to their rims. Line the bottom with a metal tray or double-strength aluminum foil to catch drainage water. Now you take it from here and add your own ideas!

Plants Warm a Summer Fireplace

To those blessed with a fireplace, there is nothing more welcome and cheerful than a crackling fire on a cold winter evening. Comes summer, however, many a fireplace turns into a large dark hole. Keeping it filled with wood, as though ready to light it, is not advised because of the danger of termites. And who wants artificial logs!

The mantel makes a natural frame for a wide, handsome container filled with pots of ferns or large-leaf philodendrons. Since there is usually little daylight in the vicinity of a fireplace, confine yourself to the most shade-loving plants. Let the style of the mantel and of the room determine the type of container. Scout the countryside and town antique shops for old copper, brass, wrought iron or wooden urns, kettles, tubs or baskets. You'll need only one, and you'll use it every summer at the fireplace—elsewhere the rest of the year—so splurge on something spectacular.

A cleverly designed bedroom for a teenager with many hobbies. Mirror-backed glass shelves are softened with trailing plants. (*Photograph courtesy of Blanche Goodman, A.S.I.D.*)

When there aren't enough art objects to fill the shelves of an etagere, plants fill up the space beautifully. The soft green of the foliage goes well with any hobby collection. (*Photograph courtesy of Window Shade Manufacturers Association*)

Plants as Hobby Collection Fillers

You've no problem if you have a handsome etagere and you've accumulated a fine collection of shells or bottles or whatever over the years. Your hobby collection is fairly extensive and easily takes up all the room you have allocated to it. But suppose you've just started a hobby collection—say Russian Easter eggs—and you've got plenty of empty space on the etagere? Those four eggs are just fabulous but they do float with all that empty space around them. Until more join their group, add plants. They won't distract from the rare beauty of the jeweled eggs, but will frame them effectively.

Have a few plants that hang, for a soft look and variety of design. Select matching, simply-designed cache-pots—plain white porcelain is perfect. As you add to the collection, take away the plants, one at a time. However, you may find that you like them so much that you'll keep a few plants anyway for the interesting texture they add to the overall composition of your hobby collection.

Plants Are a Tight Budget's Best Friends

If you're furnishing your first home or if, in a moment of wild abandon, you decided to redo the entire apartment and threw out half the furniture, it's safe to assume that you're not buying new pieces recklessly, given today's price tags on quality furnishings. It's far better, as we all know, to buy fine pieces, a few at a time, and use imagination in filling empty spaces in the meanwhile.

Plants come to the rescue in such a situation. They cost little and quickly fill up a room. Create indoor gardens in bare areas or against a wall. (See the homemade indoor planter idea discussed under *Glass walls,* pages 32 and 34) If you don't want even a temporary planter, simply group as many plants together as the area needs, assorted sizes and varieties in attractive containers (stick to one or two styles of containers). When buying plants, keep in mind the exposure of the room and how far away from the windows plants will be. A set of four snack tables can double temporarily as planters. Use them to display plants on Lucite trays. Mix in some trailing plants to hide the legs, or put tall plants on the floor.

Steps and Staircases

Rooms are frequently designed on different levels, for the break in mood and the area definition that this creates. If it's only one or two steps, this is not unpleasant to the eye; if there are more, the bare sides of the stairs may be eyesores, depending on their location in the room. If you feel that something is needed to soften the steps, group several low plants on one side, one plant in the back tall enough to "connect" the top step with the floor. On the other side, put anything *except* more plants. This would change the effect altogether and instead suggest a hotel runway with fashion models twirling in the latest styles! Try a basket filled with magazines or a whimsical ceramic animal—just use your imagination again.

Combine an Indoor Garden with an Outdoor One

An indoor-outdoor garden effect can be easily achieved if two things exist: a glass wall and a stone planter right outside the glass wall. The objec-

With floor-to-ceiling glass walls, it's easy to merge the indoors with the outdoors. For permanent displays, have low evergreens outside and house plants inside. For temporary show, have the same annuals on both sides of the glass wall, as pictured above. (*Photograph by Gottscho-Schleisner*)

tive is to give the illusion that the garden outdoors has been extended right into the living room.

This is done by building inside the same kind of planter that is outside—at the same height and of the same materials (fieldstones, slate, brick, redwood or whatever). It needn't be long, just so the eye can follow it in and out of the room. This indoor garden is best achieved in a contemporary setting where outdoor building materials are frequently utilized indoors.

Obviously the same plants can't be chosen for both planters, but they can complement one another (a uniform height of plants is important to maintain the illusion of continuity across the glass wall). If both upright and trailing plants are grown outside, a similar pattern can be repeated indoors, with different plants. Light, humidity and temperature dictate the plant material selected. More flexibility is allowed if pots are sunk into the planters instead of plants being put directly into the soil. Example: if the outside planter features trailing geraniums mixed with *Vinca major*, similar pots can be planted indoors (if one doesn't mind the extra work), both sets to be rotated every other week so that the indoor plants do not suffer too much from lack of adequate light. This plan is only for those really bent on the ultimate optical illusion and willing to give the extra time and care to achieve it.

Specimen Plants for a Touch of Drama

A specimen plant (sometimes called "accent plant") is used alone, as opposed to a grouping of several plants. It can stand by itself because it's tall, is at its peak of growth and perfection, and is unusually important-looking. This is a "star" which needs no supporting players. A good-looking but rather bland room can be brought to life with the addition of a specimen plant placed strategically. It's the "exclamation point" of a room!

A specimen plant can be a tree, a large shrub, a standard (a plant trained to a single tall stem, with a bushy head), an espalier (a fruit or other tree whose branches are trained to grow against a wall at a right angle to the main trunk) or a large, hanging basket. One can stretch this definition to include, for instance, a spectacular begonia at its peak of maturity, in a fabulous container.

The prime requisite of a specimen plant is that it be at its best stage of growth and in superb health. It should be groomed to perfection; faded flowers or dried leaves are not allowed. The condition of the plant is far more important than its rare variety. A *Dracaena marginata* is well known for its exotic dramatic effect in a room, as is that of a five-foot cactus, but equal impact on a room can be obtained with a fully mature Boston fern cascading from a basket, with a full-leaved common rubber plant, or from the popular avocado plant, if well branched. Even the wandering Jew or the spider plant is spectacular-looking when one is at its peak of growth. It's not the least bit unusual for any one of these hanging plants to span the width of an entire window and totally envelop its container.

Glorious health is imperative for specimen plants. They must be pinched, pruned, fertilized, watered properly, repotted when necessary. Obviously, any signs of pests must be attended to immediately. While it's necessary to follow these sound horticultural practices with all plants indoors, extra special care must be taken of a specimen plant if it is to perform as an important feature of the room, as would be the case with a work of art. Also not to be overlooked is that it is usually the costliest plant in the home, if it was bought when fully mature. With time and patience, you can turn one of your other handsome plants into a specimen plant.

This superb example of the mature *Dracaena marginata* needs plenty of space and a room with the handsome proportions of the one pictured. Note the fascinating shadows this plant casts on the ceiling. Depending on lighting, it can do the same against a wall. *(Photograph courtesy of Parish-Hadley, Inc.)*

The natural look of redwood paneling, plus many plants throughout the house, blend with the outdoors as seen through the walls of windows. Specimen plants are used to soften the stairs and to highlight the built-in floor planter. (*Photograph courtesy of California Redwood Association*)

What type of specimen plant to select and where to place it in the home depend on several factors: size of room, height of ceiling, amount of light, style of furnishings—and personal taste. If you think of the specimen plant as a sculpture, an art object, it will make the selection easier. To be set off properly, the plant needs plenty of room, especially if it's a tall tree or a large shrub. As a rule, plants with delicate foliage look best in traditional rooms, while those with spikes or bold, thick leaves are great for contemporary surroundings. Palms and ferns are good anywhere, making them the wonderful "classics" of the plant world. Flowering plants should only be considered where light is adequate to their needs unless, of course, the foliage alone is sufficient and the blooms are considered "leaves" if they appear. Not all flowering plants are grown strictly for their blooms. Their foliage can stand nicely on its own.

Scale is important. A small room will not take an overpowering tree. Too much foliage, and one gets the feeling of being in an overgrown jungle, reaching for the machete. Plants come in all sizes and types, so there is no reason for ending up with one that's too large or insignificant. If the walls of a room are white or pastel, the patterns made by the plant's shadow can be most effective when properly lighted. A false aralia, a *Dracaena marginata* or a Kentia palm are excellent choices for this shadow effect.

The neat, symmetrical growth habit of the Norfolk Island pine, the bold looks of the fiddle-leaf fig or of the giant dumbcane, and the twisted trunks and spikes of the *Dracaena marginata* all lend themselves to a modern room. A traditional room is a better setting for the airy softness of the various ficus trees such as *F. retusa nitida*, *F. philippinensis* or *F. benjamina exotica*. The schefflera, while large-scaled, is graceful and also well suited to the traditional room.

A specimen plant should be in keeping with the scale of the room's furnishings, as this picture illustrates most successfully. (*Photograph courtesy of House Beautiful, copyright 1973, the Hearst Corporation*)

Standards were made for stately, traditional rooms. After all, standards were born a long time ago in romantic chateaux, as an offshoot no doubt of topiary, which dates back to the Romans. I don't particularly care for topiary, but I do like the effect of a pair of standards on either side of French doors or an extra wide window. It takes a long time and a great deal of patience to grow a truly good-looking standard. But if you've ever seen a fuchsia, rose or geranium standard in full bloom, you know it's worth the effort. I have trained fuchsia, lantana, and scented geraniums into standards and have found them most rewarding. The secret is judicious pinching and pruning. This promotes lush growth, which is vital to getting that graceful "head." If they're available, buy your standards already a couple of years old so that you can place them where you want them immediately. By growing where they will remain, they'll become accustomed to that spot or will let you know soon enough! If you don't have enough light, settle for a foliage standard or do without the flowers. Most standards must be staked, so practice the art of camouflage. Use a sturdy wooden stake of a slightly larger diameter than that of the trunk of the plant. Insert it in back of the trunk and secure the two together with light brown twist-ties or wool. By having the stake and the ties almost the same color as the trunk of the plant, they will be virtually invisible.

Espaliers are dramatically beautiful when trained against the stone wall of a gallery, where the opposite wall is entirely of glass facing a sweep of lawn—but they're not for the novice gardener. Espaliers require time, constant attention and skill. A thorough knowledge of the highly specialized art of espalier pruning is imperative. The reason I even mention the subject is that there might be some readers skilled in this art form of gardening and who are looking for something "different" to grow in their atrium or glass-enclosed breezeway.

If one wishes the formal French look that espalier fruit trees give to a wall, placing several standards in a row will achieve it with far less work. If you still wish to try your hand at espaliers, the following plants are particularly suited to this form of training: orange, lemon, grapefruit, kumquat or crab-apple. For shadier spots try Japanese holly, camellias or the ever-popular *Pyracantha.*

Standards and espaliers do not take kindly to competition, which is why they are excellent as specimen plants. If you have other plants in the room, keep them at the very far end. These standards are real "stars," slow to grow and hard to train, so they deserve the limelight.

Careful thought should be given when selecting a container for a specimen plant, because both the container and the plant are on display from all angles. Containers should be deep and wide enough to accommodate the root system of the mature plants. A large clay pot with a matching saucer fits most

A room designed in a very contemporary manner needs a plant that matches its mood. Developing a feel for the "personality" of a plant is an important factor in decorating a room. (*Photograph courtesy of House Beautiful, copyright 1973, the Hearst Corporation*)

medium-sized plants, but trees and shrubs need larger containers. (Always double-pot if the container has no drainage holes.) A basket, a square wooden tub painted white or left natural (the hexagonal ones are too rustic-looking for indoor use), a porcelain urn or a ceramic planter with graceful lines are all possibilities.

If it's a flowering plant, stay away from containers that have a flower motif; select a solid color. If it's a foliage plant, and lends itself to it, then you can use a container with a design. The looks of the container should match the personality of the plant. A bold plant such as the fiddle-leaf fig looks ludicrous in a delicate porcelain cache-pot; and a graceful false aralia would be totally overpowered by a massive tub. Use your eye for scale, balance and good design. Whenever possible, purchase the plant and the container at the same time so you can see exactly how the two look together. If this isn't practical (unfortunately, at this date anyway, plants and containers are not often sold by the same store, or else they're found in two separate departments far removed from each other), at least buy them the same day, so that the appearance of each is still very vivid in your mind. Go from one to the other and use your memory to its fullest! Measure the height and diameter (across the top) of the pot the plant is in now, and buy a container that is slightly larger so that you can slip the pot right into it, allowing for some room at the bottom for a layer of pebbles. Fill space between the two pots with moss (or some other kind of mulch), adding more on the top to finish the look.

Hanging Baskets

Your spirits soar when you see mini-gardens floating in the air. This is one hanging that is fun to watch! A hanging basket displaying a full-grown, well-groomed, healthy plant is a breathtaking sight. One such basket can be the dramatic focal point of a room; several, and the room becomes a Babylonian hanging garden.

A plant is shown to its best advantage when it can be viewed from all angles. This might be called "gardening-in-the-round." It's a mini, indoor version of the outdoor "island" flower bed, which is seen from all sides as one walks around it. This extra dimension, however, allows less margin for error

This room has a lighthearted feel that is utterly charming. Hanging baskets are precisely what is needed to break up the expanse of windows and to merge with the other plants for an important grouping. (*Photograph courtesy of Window Shade Manufacturers Association*)

Warm, cozy and inviting is the way to describe this handsome contemporary home in the country. Combining many floor plants with lush hanging baskets, a striking indoor garden is created—ideal for floor-to-ceiling glass walls. (*Photograph by Gottscho-Schleisner*)

when decorating with hanging baskets. Unless plants are kept in tip-top shape, it's best to forget the whole idea. But it would be a great loss because hanging baskets add warmth and charm to a room and, besides, take no space other than "air rights." This is an important factor in small rooms, but even where space is not at a premium, the loveliness and romantic aura that hanging plants contribute are sufficient reasons to grow them. There are few requirements for the successful culture of hanging plants, but these are important.

Location. As mentioned in the Window Treatments chapter, windows, alcoves, bay windows and glass walls are all naturals for hanging plants. Plants can also do double duty, screening out unattractive views such as an adjoining building, a neighbor's picture window or terrace looking into yours, and other problems. Flowering plants require a lot of sun, so windows are logical locations. Save foliage plants for the shadier spots in the home.

Other areas where hanging plants are effective are stairwells and stair landings (if there is a window or skylight), enclosed porches, hallways where the front door is flanked by glass panels—in short, any place where there is sufficient light for a plant to grow. Plants can be hung just about anywhere in a sunny room that has lots of windows or glass walls, with the shade-loving ones farthest from the windows and those needing the most sun right in front of the windows. If a plant grows well in a particular spot in the room, there is no reason to doubt that it can thrive equally well in that location if it's suspended from a chain. Obviously, this excludes spots with blasts of air coming from air conditioners or heating outlets placed high up the wall.

How to hang plants. This is a matter of proportion and balance, similar to grouping plants anywhere else. Here are some guidelines: Hang plants at eye level. This makes sense not only for watering and caring for the plant, but also for admiring it. If you must throw your head backward and go into contortions to see a plant, it's badly hung. Chains are sold by the yard, so it's easy to have as long or short a length as is needed to put the plant at a comfortable height. I often wonder how hanging plants are watered and groomed in magazine photographs where they're suspended close to the ceiling of a cavernous room. Visions of fire-ladders come to my mind, in order to reach these celestial plants! When you are hanging plants in a stairwell, "eye" level obviously depends on what part of the stairs you're standing on, so pick the most attractive angle as long as you can easily water and care for the plants without falling several flights below.

Plants shouldn't be so crowded that their foliage intermingles, least of all hanging plants, which require plenty of space to be fully appreciated. When grouping several plants, leave space between them but keep them close enough together to form a unit, and hang them at varying heights. The "cascade" look is done by connecting a plant to the one above or placing several hooks in the ceiling, close together, with chains of different lengths, measured in such a way that each plant picks up where another ends. Even though this gives the illusion of one long column of greens, proper spacing will prevent plants from touching each other. Leave room for plants to grow, and when plants finally do merge, pinch them back (which should be done anyway) to keep within bounds.

Don't despair if you feel you're not with it simply because you still have glass curtains on the windows. The trend in interior design may be away from curtains to different window treatments, but from the point of view of plants, they couldn't be happier. Sheer curtains screen out the burning rays of the intense summer sun, and in winter, curtains keep the chill away. Windows with southern exposures need some sort of screen to prevent plants on glass shelves, or hanging in front of the window, from getting cooked in summer. But whatever form of covering is used on the window, it should be sheer enough to allow light to come through. If the shade, the venetian blind or the curtain shuts out all light, the plants might just as well be in a closet.

If you must hang plants in a totally bare window devoid of any screening, choose trailing varieties of plants that thrive in this type of climate. Sedums, cacti and succulents are accustomed to extreme heat in daytime and sudden cold at night. In any case, plants should never be allowed to touch the glass panes. Glass intensifies the outside temperature, and it's easy to burn or freeze delicate foliage.

The weight of the plant is an important factor to consider when looking around the home for places to hang it. A plant weighs pounds more after being watered. Check to see that your walls and ceilings can take it. Transparent plastic pots in handsome rope hangers are the lightest containers you can use. Also, consider soilless mixes as potting soil, but remember that a regular fertilizing program must be followed to supply the plants with the necessary nutrients, making this method of gardening more time-consuming.

Wrought iron brackets, or their modern counterparts made of clear Lucite, need especially long screws to offset the weight dangling from their tips. Screws which come with many brackets are seldom long or strong enough, so it's wise to buy your own. Ask your hardware dealer about nylon and metal expansion anchors (the "Molly" is well-known). These provide the holding power needed for hanging baskets, either from the ceiling or from a bracket on the wall.

Selecting containers. There are several factors to keep in mind. The first is the growth habit of the plant. If it grows rapidly (like the wandering Jew) until it completely hides the pot, there's no need to spend a lot of money on a container that won't be seen. A clear or bronze-tinted transparent plastic pot with matching saucer will disappear under the plant. So will the rope hanger that holds pot and saucer together. Ivies and wandering Jews are good examples of plants that form a thick cascade of leaves, completely hiding their containers when fully mature.

If the plant to be displayed has yet to reach its full maturity or if it's a variety that will always have airy foliage, then the container as well as the plant is "on stage." It's no longer enough that the container be functional; appearance becomes important and should be kept in mind when you are looking over the vast array of hanging containers available today.

Another factor to consider is the type of container that is best for the plant from the horticultural point of view. Only one with drainage holes should be used, along with a matching saucer, or you can double-pot the plant into a handsome waterproof container. As already mentioned, potting a plant directly into a container without holes is a constant guessing game of how much water to give and how much may still remain at the bottom. This is not fair to the plant and it is hard on your nerves. Since hanging plants dry out much more quickly than others, and since weight is a factor, use a lightweight plastic pot rather than a clay one when double-potting. Don't forget that the layer of pebbles at the bottom of the outer container adds still more weight to the whole thing. Repeat the mulch idea as for other double-potted plants (see page 18) to hide the inner pot. If in doubt as to whether or not the outer container is entirely waterproof, put a saucer at the bottom or line it with heavy plastic or aluminum foil before adding pebbles. The principle of double-potting plants in jardinieres or cache-pots can be applied to any hanging plant.

There's a third factor to remember if you're grouping several hanging plants. The same principle applies as with containers on the ground: don't attempt to mix more than two styles of containers in the same room. Naturally, this applies to plants whose growth habit allows the container to be seen clearly; if plants completely hide their containers, any container can be chosen so long as it has good drainage.

Hang several plants in identical pots, adding one spectacular plant in a very handsome jardiniere. (Remember that a jardiniere is any waterproof container into which you put the plant, pot and all.) If the jardiniere doesn't come with its own hanging rope, buy a colorful one that blends or accents the jardiniere. Example: take a Boston fern in its plastic pot, place it inside an attractive basket (adding a saucer at the bottom), and suspend the whole thing by a brown or natural-color rope hanger. The mellow earth tones of the basket and the hanger go well with ferns. Glazed pots held by leather ropes are goodlooking with trailing cacti or succulents. There are many imaginative possibilities, but don't mix them together. One touch of drama per plant grouping is sufficient.

Once you fulfill the basic requirements of soil and pot, what kind of outer container you put the plant in depends on your imagination, taste, availability of containers locally and amount of money you wish to spend. The style of your room's furnishings plays a key role in selecting a container. You wouldn't want a clay bowl for a formal English or French room. A simple porcelain or glazed ceramic pot is more in keeping. There are sleek, modern "baskets" for contemporary homes. The new plastic or Plexiglas baskets are goodlooking for double-potting. Line the basket with moss before putting in the plant in its pot, so that all you see through the transparent basket is the moss and the plant—the inner pot is hidden from view. If you insist on planting directly into a waterproof transparent plastic basket, make up for the lack of drainage holes by filling it at least one-third with pebbles before adding the potting mix, to which an extra dose of sand or Perlite has been added

to insure adequate drainage. I also suggest choosing plants that need above-average watering, to further minimize the chance of root rot. When using glass or metal containers, keep them out of direct sunlight and line them with moss to retain coolness. We all know what happens when the sun hits glass—a cooked plant can be the result!

Two of the most popular hanging planters are best left for outdoor use: the moss-lined wire basket and the slatted redwood basket. The first one is the most natural-looking container for a plant, but also the messiest. The moss, once dried, constantly sheds on the floor. It has to be double-potted or else the soil will drain out bit by bit with each watering. Even outdoors, where I use these planters exclusively, I double-pot, because the dehydration is intense during the summer months and an inner plastic pan is a big help in retaining moisture. If the house plant is put directly into the basket, without benefit of pot, then the whole thing should be submerged in water at least once a week—and that's a job! Outdoors, it's a simple matter to use the garden hose.

The basket made of slatted redwood is also best left for outdoors, for the very same reasons. Anyway, it's too rustic-looking for most rooms and looks its best when hung under trees. I also double-pot these baskets, filling in the empty spaces and the surface with moss.

Possibly the most frequently seen basket is of white or green metal with an attached saucer. I personally don't find this style attractive, but more important, the saucer is inadequate. It's not nearly large enough to catch all the drainage water. Most houseplants should be watered until water comes out the bottom. When this is done to a plant in this type of basket, the water inevitably overflows all over the floor. So either use this basket as an inner container for a waterproof jardiniere, or save it for outside use. The ideal basket, which would be a decorative asset to a room, with adequate drainage holes and a sufficiently deep attached saucer, has yet to be designed. In the meantime, use your imagination and combine colorful rope hangers with goodlooking waterproof planters to hold the plant in its own plain plastic or clay pot. Beauty and horticultural needs are both served successfully.

Where informality is the mood, it's fun to search for offbeat containers

Hanging baskets don't always have to "hang." They can be fastened to a wall, as shown here. Brick and stone are the best backgrounds. Mix varieties of plants to avoid monotony. Give thought to placement as carefully as you would to grouping paintings on a wall. (*Photograph by Gottscho-Schleisner*)

that are conversation pieces. I've already mentioned the wire mesh salad basket to hold pots of chives or variegated ivies in the kitchen. There's also a three-tier hanger of wire mesh bowls, each of which can hold one good-sized hanging plant, making a stunning hanging garden. Hung from the ceiling in front of a sunny window, this three-tier arrangement makes a great herb garden. Or, if you prefer a solid cascade of greens, put in pots of your favorite fancy ivy (with saucers under the pots, naturally) and you'll have the charm of fresh green foliage all year long. Keep the weight of these three-tier gardens in mind, however. If necessary, rig up a double suspension installation. It's nothing more than putting two identical brackets parallel on the wall, or two hooks in the ceiling, and looping the chain around both. This distributes the weight between two supports instead of one, and is a help when hanging anything extra-heavy.

Are saucers needed? Yes, yes, yes! I can't stress enough the need for saucers under pots, *all* pots, but especially in hanging baskets. It's easy to see the reason for this. We already know that to water a plant properly, enough water should be given to drain some out the bottom. Depending on many factors—size of root ball, type of soil, temperature, etc.—a little or a great deal of water may fill the saucer. If the saucer is too small or shallow, it quickly overflows. Many plant owners, fearing this, water very sparingly, a few drops every day or so, and wonder why their plants are not thriving. A good drenching once a week is better than a daily sprinkling.

If a hanging plant is double-potted, there is no problem with drainage. A thin layer of pebbles at the bottom of the outer pot prevents the roots of the plant from rotting as a result of "sitting" in water too long. However, do not be afraid of a little bit of water at the bottom. Most plants will take a second drink by absorbing more water slowly, and evaporation in warmer weather takes care of the rest. My hanging baskets and other double-potted plants are in excellent health, although they are always sitting in an inch of water after I get through watering them. A day or so later, all the water in the outer pot or in the saucer has completely disappeared. Obviously, I wouldn't allow this amount of water to stand for several days or a week, but I repeat, a day or two does no harm. Since cacti and related plant families should be watered very sparingly, this accumulation of water does not occur and therefore presents no problem.

Here is a way to test a plant's water absorption ability in order to prevent disasters on your precious antique rug. Take the hanging plant and saucer to kitchen sink. Water the plant thoroughly until the first sign of water comes out the bottom. Let it stand for ten minutes. If water overflows, you need a larger saucer. If it's only about halfway up the saucer, then it's the right size and you can put pot and saucer in the rope hanger and suspend it where you want. If you're still nervous, play safe and double-pot it.

Window sills, when deep enough, are naturals for holding plants. Note that radiator grills are not *under* the plants but face into the room. This grouping of plants forms a handsome background for the couch. (*Photograph courtesy of Window Shade Manufacturers Association*)

ABOVE: The extra-wide window in the author's apartment bedroom has a permanently installed air conditioner which cuts out a great deal of light. Nevertheless, plants chosen for low-light requirements thrive on top of the radiator (which is never turned on). Plants hide side panels of the air conditioner and are kept below the front grills from which the air flows. (*Photograph by Brian Manning*)

OPPOSITE: It's winter outside, but indoors potted bulbs bring a promise of spring. Their vivid colors brighten any room. Group several pots together for maximum effect. (*Photograph by Malak of Ottawa*)

It's hard to top the charm of a bay window filled with assorted plants. The lushness of the greenery makes it difficult to tell where indoors and outdoors separate. (*Photograph courtesy of McMillen Inc.*)

ABOVE: When not in use, the air conditioner (left) in the author's city apartment is completely hidden. During the summer, only the hanging plants on either side are left, as well as the upright plants on top of the appliance. Air flows from the front of the air conditioner, so that plants on top and sides are not affected. (*Photograph by Brian Manning*)

BELOW: The outdoors is brought right into the house, creating a break in a long wall of glass. The plant stand and the floor tray are in keeping with the mood and style of the room. (*Photograph courtesy of McMillen Inc.*)

ABOVE: Simplicity is the keynote of this quiet corner. The plant is the strong accent, gracefully framing the window. (*Photograph courtesy of Parish-Hadley Inc.*)

OPPOSITE: The high humidity in bathrooms is beneficial to plants. Mirrors and plants enlarge this small bathroom. Lights must be kept on all day. (*Interior design by Stephen Heidrich of Hoffman & Heidrich, in conjunction with Ray Tomkin*)

ABOVE: The formal elegance of this living room is heightened in the winter by a cheerful fire and in the summer by a grouping of ferns in the fireplace. The palm is moved away from the fire's heat in the winter. (*Apartment of interior designer Dick Ridge; photograph by Brian Manning*)

OPPOSITE: Long, narrow, galley-type kitchens are typical of city apartments. The single window usually faces a blank wall, as does the one above, but this picture dramatically illustrates what can be done with such a kitchen. Glass shelves across the window hold herbs and other plants. Much-needed additional light comes from fluorescent tubes at the top and sides of the window. (*Apartment of interior designer Dick Ridge; photograph by Brian Manning*)

ABOVE: The boldness and exotic beauty of a giant cactus make it a living sculpture, especially effective in rooms of oriental mood or Southwestern style. (*Photograph courtesy of Edith Gecker, F.N.S.I.D.*)

OPPOSITE: It's easy to see why the *Dracaena marginata* has long been a favorite accent plant of designers. Its unusual branching habit and strong leaf-spikes have a dramatic impact on a room. It's a plant to use strictly alone. (*Photograph courtesy of Parish-Hadley Inc.*)

ABOVE: Specimen trees look almost like hanging baskets from afar, with only their "heads" left on—the perfect choice for tall twin windows. (*Rex Reed residence by interior designer Dick Ridge*)

OPPOSITE: The kitchen flows right into an attached greenhouse. Use of similar flooring material further unites the two areas. Extra caution should be taken, however, to make sure that adequate drainage exists under the greenhouse floor to prevent rot of the house foundation. A small pool against the side wall makes it possible to grow water plants, and the fountain increases the humidity. It's a lovely spot to sip morning coffee while reading the paper and listening to the bird sing in its cage. Bamboo blinds hide pots and working material under the benches. (*Connecticut residence of Mr. and Mrs. James Chapin; photograph by Brian Manning*)

ABOVE: This striking, contemporary, glass-enclosed dining room combines many principles in the effective use of plants. Empty space beside the steps is filled in with a grouping of plants. A stone planter serves as a dramatic divider between the dining room and the rest of the house. Begonias cascading from the planter flow beautifully into the plants grouped on the floor. (*Residence of Mr. and Mrs. Franklin Schaffer, Greenwich, Connecticut; photograph by Brian Manning*)

OPPOSITE: An atrium is technically not a greenhouse because temperature and humidity can't be controlled, but it's usually much cooler and more humid than the rest of the house, and thus is ideal for plants. Light comes from above, through the roof, or from the sides as in these photographs. This atrium also receives additional light through glass walls which face Long Island Sound. Permanent, year-round plants are supplemented by pots of seasonal flowers. Floor drainage and a hose connected to a water faucet make it easy to water the many plants and to spray the gravel to increase humidity. A magnificent indoor garden is as much a part of the interior design of this home as are all the furniture and accessories. (*Residence of Mr. and Mrs. Robert F. Walmsley; photograph by Brian Manning*)

The high ceiling and tall window of the author's bathroom are typical of those found in older city apartments. Such large windows are perfect for displaying hanging baskets. Glass curtains, which are necessary for privacy, also screen out burning rays of the summer sun. When the top of the window or ceiling can't take hooks for baskets, the heavy brass rod shown is one solution to the problem. Plants on the wicker tray help to distract the eye from the washing machine. (*Photograph by Brian Manning*)

Don't assume that all plants drink water the same way, even plants that are alike. Factors already mentioned play a part, as does the age of the plant. The older the plant, the larger the root ball, usually, and therefore the less soil in the pot. This in turn means that the water quickly drains through. Some of my largest baskets drain in no time, reminding me that it's getting near the time to repot the plants in a larger size or root-prune them in the same pot. (See page 211 for root-pruning.) With others, I have to keep adding water until I finally see it come out the bottom. If you really care for your mature plants, and want to postpone the repotting bit, empty the saucer of excess water into a pail, and water the plant again, several times, emptying the saucer as it fills up. In my opinion this is easier than lifting a large, heavy basket to the bathtub and soaking it for fifteen minutes, and then letting it dry thoroughly before rehanging. There's also the danger of bruising the underpart of the plant as it sits in the tub. Older baskets are as full underneath as they are on top, and trying to put one down anywhere without breaking off stems is quite a trick. I gave up trying to transport these full baskets from my greenhouse in the country to my apartment in town. Instead, I brought in small plants and let them grow to a ripe old age right in the city, where they never moved once I discovered which spot they're happiest in.

Because nothing is 100 percent foolproof in spite of all the precautions one might take, it's best to carry a terry towel around when you water hanging baskets. You never know when one will overflow, and if you can quickly mop up and spread a towel underneath the basket, you'll save your rug and keep your temper down. Some plants are not above playing tricks! I have one which looks as though it has taken in all the water I gave it, with nary a drop showing in the saucer. If I hadn't learned the hard way, I would keep adding more water, which would be a calamity, because the dear little plant takes its own good time. It eventually fills up the saucer right to the rim. Only *you* can get to know your plants and their habits and establish a routine. However, you might try these guidelines as a starter.

What to plant. The chapter on plant material (pages 198-206) gives a list of easy-to-grow trailing plants, but before checking this information, go over some of the points below.

1. When hanging several baskets together in one area, select plants that have the same cultural requirements. If it's a sunny window, have only plants requiring lots of light. Group the shade-loving ones together elsewhere.

2. Keep in mind the effect you wish to create with hanging baskets. To shut out a view? Choose large, full-leaved varieties that grow tightly, allowing very little to be seen through them, such as ivies and wandering Jews. Do you want a long, cascading, rippling effect? There are plants that grow and grow and grow! Select from those. Want a romantic, light, airy look? There are lots, including the hard-to-kill asparagus fern. Before choosing a plant, think first what you want it to do and then select accordingly, always bearing in mind, naturally, its cultural needs.

3. To mix or not? If you are hanging three baskets, should you have three ivies, or one ivy, one begonia, and one asparagus fern? Personal choice may be the deciding factor, but again, it's back to the effect you wish to create. If you want a massive "jungle look" of greenery, several baskets of the same lush variety, such as ferns or ivies, will do the job. But you can avoid the possibility of monotony, without sacrificing the end result, by having different varieties of the same type of plant. There are countless varieties of ivies, ferns, begonias, and so forth. Select one "family" of plants, and introduce several varieties within that family, so long as they have the same growth habits and cultural requirements.

If, on the other hand, you have a bay window or a glass wall and you want a "hanging garden," you need different plant families to create changes in textures, colors, forms. Combining foliage plants with flowering ones makes for good contrast, each setting off the other. However, keep your eye alert for balance in the overall design. Don't mix a tiny basket with several very large ones because it will simply get lost. Keep small baskets together, reserving the extra-wide mature ones as individual specimens in windows—one to a window. Of course, if you have a very long glass wall, as found in many contemporary homes, it's very dramatic to hang all your large plants together. There'll still be enough room between them to allow them to breathe properly and to be shown off effectively.

When hanging baskets, think of them as you would paintings on a wall. You display paintings in such a way that one does not clash with the other—close enough together to form a design, yet allowing just enough space to separate each from the others. Color is as important in grouping plants as in grouping paintings. Plants of pale foliage are most effective when placed next to those of rich, deep greens. Example: the dark green of grape ivy is a perfect foil for the striped ivory and light green of the variegated spider plant. Also, avoid hanging baskets at precisely the same height. Staggering them slightly gives a graceful natural look.

4. Should you plant more than one kind of plant in the same basket? I don't much care for the idea because I think crowding too many plants into one pot is simply not good for them. I know it's done for quick effect by many florists, but for long-term growing it's not a wise idea. But you can compromise and create a simply fantastic one-basket garden by surrounding an upright growing plant with green trailing foliage. The new, large-flowered begonias teamed with ivy make a good combination. White or pale pink flowers go best with green foliage, the rich reds and purples having a tendency to merge with the leaves surrounding them.

Geraniums edged with *Vinca major* have been a standby for years. The trouble is that neither does very well indoors, and when the geraniums are not in bloom the two types of foliage don't make a particularly handsome combination. But if you find yourself successful in growing these two plants, by all means combine them for a sunny window.

Not all baskets must contain long, trailing plants. When making your selection, consider plants of upright growth habits as well. However, they should be full and bushy. Tall, spindly plants won't do. Many begonias which are not technically hanging plants do superbly in baskets. They have a spreading habit, their colorful foliage is striking, and the stems curve downward just enough to be especially suited to baskets. But be sure not to hang them above eye level. Let these baskets be the lower ones in your hanging arrangement. Rex begonias and other non-trailing plants must be seen at eye level or slightly below to be properly appreciated. To conserve bench space in my greenhouse, I suspended many begonias and discovered how much better they were displayed that way. Wax begonias do not lend themselves to this treatment because they are too erect in their growth habit. But you can compensate for this by surrounding them with trailing ivy. Begonias have relatively small root balls and so can be teamed with other plants in the same pot without suffering damage.

I have never been able to grow *impatiens* successfully indoors, although I have masses of them outside and in the greenhouse. But if you find yourself able to keep them blooming inside, plant them with ivy. I have several tubs of this combination on the terrace, under the awning in summer, and it gives a very lush effect. *Impatiens* are well-branched and bushy, with beautiful foliage and brilliantly hued flowers, so that they "fill" a basket handsomely. Ivy around them finishes off the "hanging garden." Several of these baskets in a heated sunporch would cheer the gloomiest winter days. *Impatiens* are shade-loving plants, but the weak winter sun won't displease them.

The Greenhouse as an Extra Living Room

Time was that when the word "greenhouse" was mentioned, thoughts of vast estates came to mind, with head gardeners and their assistants, extravagant heating bills and hundreds of exotic plants tenderly groomed for the sole purpose of filling the house with fabulous fresh flowers daily. Or a greenhouse simply meant a commercial enterprise growing plants and flowers for resale purposes. This latter type of greenhouse obviously still exists, more successful than ever, but the grandiose private model is fast dwindling into history.

Today's greenhouse belongs to the dedicated hobbyist who has discovered a whole new world of deep satisfaction and pleasure. It's his home-away-from-home and takes a great deal of his time to maintain—all of which he loves dearly, for he is a serious gardener. But a new category of greenhouse has emerged in the last few years, one that is looked upon as an integral part of the house, an extra "living" room in the true sense. This type of greenhouse is not so much for growing plants as it is for enjoying daily life *among* plants. It's not only attached to the house, but frequently its fourth wall is nonexistent—in that there are no doors leading from the greenhouse into the house. One just walks straight from the greenhouse into the kitchen, or the living room, or whatever. This unity is further emphasized when the flooring of the greenhouse matches that of the connecting room.

A greenhouse-room has comfortable terrace furniture of wicker, wrought iron or canvas. One can read, watch TV, entertain friends, read the morning paper with that second cup of coffee. When snow covers the ground outside and the trees are depressingly bare, it's a glorious feeling to be surrounded by flowers one wouldn't ordinarily see for several more months.

One might very well ask what the difference is between a greenhouse-room and an enclosed sunporch. First is the construction: it's definitely built as a lean-to greenhouse, with vents, glass roof and sides that can go straight to the ground level or stand on a concrete foundation, as desired. The greenhouse-room has a water outlet and drainage in the floor. It has a built-in bench along three of its walls for holding plants (this is optional). Heating can be via a separate unit or directly connected to the house.

This greenhouse-room requires help and guidance in building from professionals in the greenhouse field. It can be kept simple or filled with elaborate

Is this a greenhouse used as a living area, or a delightful kitchen-dinette with a greenhouse cover? It's a happy blend of both. How many or how few plants to have in ratio to the furniture is a matter of personal choice. The vast expanse of glass permits cultivation of many flowering plants, but since there can be no control over climate, selection of plants is obviously far more limited than would be allowed in a regular greenhouse. This is more than made up for, however, by the fact that the room can be used for regular day-to-day living. For those who love the outdoors so much that they'd like it to come right into the house, a greenhouse-living room is a dream come true. (*Photograph courtesy of House Beautiful, copyright 1973, the Hearst Corporation*)

gadgets, as the budget allows. A separate thermostat is a must, however, and automatically-controlled vents are appreciated to supply adequate ventilation based on the widely fluctuating temperatures. When the sun hits those glass panels, the temperature even in mid-winter can soar into the eighties or higher, and then drop sharply at night. Humidity is also an important factor, but you won't be able to control it as you would in a "working greenhouse," since the area opens directly into the house.

Just a few steps down from the living room, in full view, is another world—an indoor garden under glass. Shades screen the sun in summer, needed to maintain airconditioning on a proper level. Because of the bright light, house plants thrive better than they would in other parts of the house. The massive grouping of greenery is a dramatic setting for the living room. (*Photograph courtesy of Lord & Burnham*)

Too many people are under the impression that only those who love to garden and are skilled at it can have such a room. This is not so. It is simply a dramatic way of displaying plants—home-grown or not—and of enjoying being surrounded by them. The decorative impact of such a mass of flowers and greenery when seen from inside the house is tremendous. It is an area of vivid colors and cool greens which brings an added dimension to everyday living.

There are several ways of displaying plants in a greenhouse-room, but the most practical is a built-in redwood bench around the three sides of the structure, which you fill with gravel. Planting directly into soil is not for this type of greenhouse. It's easier to stick to container gardening. Keeping the gravel constantly moist raises the humidity to a level more pleasing to the plants, yet not uncomfortable for people. Special brackets which hold glass shelves can be added to the greenhouse walls, providing additional space for plants. Only a small area of the bench need be reserved for growing cuttings, nursing sick plants and for general care and grooming of plants. Space under the bench is reserved for storage of pots and plastic garbage cans holding potting soil mixes, pesticides, tools, and so forth. These can be hidden from view with roll-up bamboo blinds. Or cabinets can be built under the bench.

How many and what kind of plants to grow depend on personal choice and the size of your room, but there should be enough to make one feel that he is sitting in a quiet corner of a garden, a peaceful oasis of nature. Have at least one important tree or tall shrub on the floor, with a mixture of foliage and flowering plants on the bench. Since this is a room to be lived in, there is not much leeway regarding temperature. A "cool" greenhouse (which runs from 45 to 50 degrees—"intermediate" goes from 50 to 60) would not be comfortable except during sunny days, and evenings would be far too cold. Also, it should be noted that since this area is usually open to the rest of the house, the temperature in it cannot be strictly controlled. A "warm" greenhouse, meaning night temperatures of from 60 to 70 degrees, allows you to grow delightful plants while remaining comfortable. The energy crisis is a factor to consider in those parts of the country dependent on fuel oil. Having an electric heater for cool evenings is a help, in which case the "intermediate" zone would be feasible. But no matter what plants you grow at what temperature, you may be sure that they will fare far better than they would in other rooms. Even though the environment is not strictly that of a regular greenhouse, there are enough of the latter's benefits to be sheer heaven to your plants.

If there is room, think about adding a fountain or a small pool. You can create a delightful woodland garden in one corner of the greenhouse-room by surrounding the edge of the pool or the base of the fountain with ferns and moisture-loving plants like umbrella plant, spathiphyllum, sweet flag, baby's-

A window greenhouse can be installed in as many windows as one wishes. But whether it's one window or four, as shown above and on the opposite page, it provides lots of display area for plants without taking up any space inside the house or city terrace. Note the pebbles on bottom shelves to catch dripping water from all the plants above. Top windows open out for ventilation. ***(Photographs courtesy of Lord & Burnham and Gottscho-Schleisner)***

tears, rex begonias, etc. A sunken pot of water lilies finishes the look. Cover the surface of the pot with a good layer of sand and small pebbles to prevent soil from floating away underwater. Make the pool look as natural as possible by edging it with rocks and filling the crevices with moss.

A greenhouse-room is not only for house owners. One can be enjoyed by apartment dwellers who have a terrace. By enclosing the terrace, or part of it, the same results can be achieved. But as with any architectural changes made in a home, it's important to check local building and zoning codes, or the landlord in the case of a rented apartment.

Since gardening is not the prime objective in this type of greenhouse, exposure is not a serious consideration. South and east exposures are best for flowering plants, but there are enough foliage plants to take care of shadier locations. In any case, I feel that too much fuss is made over greenhouse exposures, thereby discouraging many people from building one and enjoying a whole new world. Nature is not nearly so particular. She covers the gamut from dry, sunny climates to dark jungle forests, and manages to have vegetation growing almost everywhere, in happy ignorance.

Cut down on the excessive summer heat with shades, either those specially made for greenhouses or roll-up bamboo shades. I've used the latter for years and find them very attractive. They don't last more than a couple of years but are so inexpensive that it doesn't really matter. Raise the humidity by keeping the pebbles in the bench moist, or if you keep the plants on the floor and on tables, put them on saucers which are filled with pebbles. Keeping these moist will help tremendously. Obviously a fountain or a pool will also contribute to higher humidity. Keep fresh air circulating, either through automatic or manually operated vents.

These three factors—heat, humidity and ventilation—are important to remember, but since you and your family will be using the room as well as the plants, chances are you'll strike a proper balance. Many plants don't like extreme heat or cold any more than people do. A humidifier is useful, not only for plants but for people and furniture as well. A hygrometer is an essential gadget that tells you how much humidity there is in the air. Hosing down the flooring to clean it will automatically raise the humidity. In very hot weather it's a good idea to do this every day. If you want area rugs on the floor to keep it warmer in winter, get indoor-outdoor carpeting, straw mats or similar all-weather materials. Since greenhouse flooring is usually of bricks, tiles, slate or concrete squares, all of which are cold underfoot, some covering is needed during cold weather.

It should be stressed at this point that you shouldn't expect the same type of results with plants from your greenhouse-room that your friends have with their full-fledged greenhouses which are scientifically controlled for optimum horticultural requirements. You will be severely restrained as to pesticides that you may use, since the area to be sprayed is part of the house. Only chemicals which are safe to use inside the home should be used. Read labels carefully to make certain of this. Since the purpose of this room is to function as a "garden living room," allowances have to be made. But this much you can count on. Your plants will thrive far better in this environment than they will anywhere else in the house. It is, in effect, a sort of "halfway" house for them: better than an average room would be, yet not quite as perfect as a regular greenhouse.

Wicker clothes hampers and large wicker baskets with lids make excellent containers to store all the material and accessories needed to keep plants well-groomed and healthy. Put soil mixtures in large plastic bags inside the hampers, as well as extra pots and saucers. Fertilizers, sprays, shard for drainage, mulch material and so forth can all go inside the baskets. Keep them under the benches or behind a grouping of tall plants on the floor—or use them as stands for plants when not in use! Naturally, as mentioned earlier, you can have open shelves or cabinets built to order under the bench. The wicker hamper idea is suggested primarily for those situations where a bench does not exist and plants are displayed on tables and stands instead. In my "working greenhouse" potting shed, I use wicker baskets to hold all those little items that get lost so easily, such as "twist-ems" (ties to stake plants), measuring spoons for fertilizers, small hand tools for pot use, scissors, sharp knives, cotton swabs, etc.

Careful grooming of plants is vital since they are on display all the time, as are the other plants in the house. Since this is a "showcase" greenhouse, pots and containers should be kept clean, as should the pebbles on the bench. These need periodic raking and leveling, easily done with a toy rake. Red clay pots look best when so many plants are grouped together. The mellow color of clay is never jarring to the eye. Add matching saucers to the large pots on the floor. Trees and shrubs require the larger-sized redwood tubs. There are round green tubs which are also excellent and which make colorful accents against white wicker furniture.

We've been discussing a room-sized greenhouse, but as small an area as a window can be turned into a tiny greenhouse and become the dramatic focal point of a room. It's a space-saving way to show off a collection of choice plants. There are prefabricated models which you can install yourself or have done for you. Additional space is not required, since the greenhouse is built outside the window. (There's nothing to stop you from building one outside several adjoining windows for a really fantastic effect!)

The three outer sides and the top of the greenhouse are glass, with vents in the top and at the bottom of the sides for ventilation. Glass shelves hold plants across the window, and a galvanized tray accommodates more at the bottom. Setting the plants on trays with a layer of moistened pebbles increases the humidity. Screens keep out insects, and adding an electric soil cable prevents plants from getting chilled on exceptionally cold winter nights. (Glass intensifies outside temperatures.)

As with the larger greenhouse-room, plants which normally could not be grown successfully elsewhere in the house will thrive in a window greenhouse, because of the extra sunlight and the tighter control that is possible over ventilation, temperature and humidity. By checking with a thermometer and a hygrometer, more nearly ideal conditions can be achieved to meet the plants' cultural requirements. If the window greenhouse is left open to the room (as opposed to having the window act as a door or fourth side), it will be more difficult to regulate the mini-climate inside, as is the case with the greenhouse-room; but it will be far more attractive to the eye. Looking at plants from outside a windowpane dilutes much of the charm and warmth that plants contribute to a setting. They appear relegated to a clinical-laboratory status, appropriate to the commercial and educational worlds, but not inside one's home.

For anyone interested in this type of indoor gardening, I strongly recommend sending for brochures from greenhouse manufacturers (see pages 226-232). These are experts in the field, who not only sell their products but give guidance in proper selection and correct installation—together with definitive suggestions about which plants to grow for specific temperature-humidity ranges.

Gardens Under Artificial Lights

Next to owning his own greenhouse, the avid gardener cherishes having an indoor area where he can grow plants under artificial lights all year long. The former can be costly, but the latter is within the budget of anyone. Until recently, this type of indoor gardening was primarily for people who wanted to get an early start in growing their flowers and vegetables before setting them outdoors. It was also for hobbyists who wanted to get flowers at a time of year when ordinarily plants would not bloom.

Gardening under artificial lights has been a no-nonsense endeavor. Fixtures have no frills and no concern for appearance. This kind of gardening started in the basement, where the gardener set up his benches or tables holding flats of seeds, with light fixtures overhead. It progressed to kitchen counters and other places hidden from the more formal rooms of the home.

Considering the popularity of growing indoor plants, it is amazing that even today so few fixtures are manufactured that can be decorative as well as functional. Of course, if one works through an interior decorator, one can have stunning made-to-order installations with all the necessary accessories neatly hidden. However, judging from ads which are appearing more frequently, there should be increasingly more lighting fixtures and planters on the market which will enable the homeowner to bring his artificial equipment into the open and not have to apologize for it. The U.S. Department of Agriculture has an excellent pamphlet available, Number 187, which has designs for do-it-yourself installations.

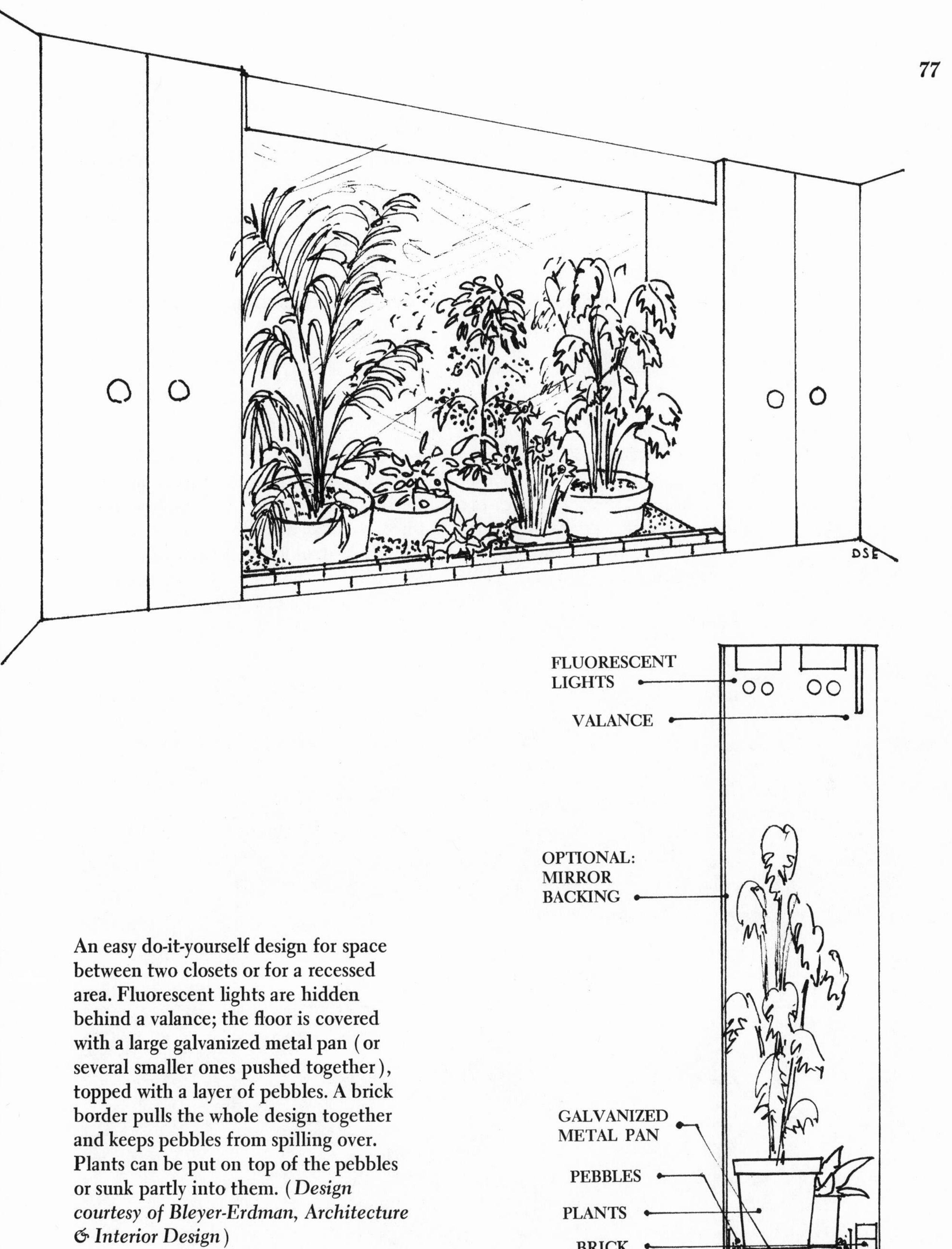

An easy do-it-yourself design for space between two closets or for a recessed area. Fluorescent lights are hidden behind a valance; the floor is covered with a large galvanized metal pan (or several smaller ones pushed together), topped with a layer of pebbles. A brick border pulls the whole design together and keeps pebbles from spilling over. Plants can be put on top of the pebbles or sunk partly into them. (*Design courtesy of Bleyer-Erdman, Architecture & Interior Design*)

In this book, our chief interest in gardening under artificial lights is to enable us to grow plants in areas of the home that normally would be out of the question. Without adequate light, plants simply won't grow and it's frequently in dark, out-of-the-way spots that plants are most welcome to decorate areas not large enough for furniture.

Entire books have been written on the subject of gardening under lights and I recommend that you read one if you wish to go into greater depth. (See Bibliography, page 234.)

Where can you grow plants under lights? Anywhere that is too dark for

It's rare to find such a graceful-looking fixture for artificial lighting. Clean lines and simplicity make this one appropriate for most homes. It can be used alone or fitted on cabinet shelves, bookcases or etageres; a similar model, without legs, can be used as a shelf light. Grouping two or three makes an attractive garden area. It's best to set plants on trays filled with pebbles. Matching wood trays with waterproof liners are available. This model features two 20-watt Vita-Lite lamps and can be connected to a timer. There is a choice of walnut wood grain, white or colors. (*Photograph courtesy of Fleco Industries, Dallas, Texas*)

Hiding lamps and trays is the chief problem of indoor gardeners who demand beauty with the functional. There are several ways of solving this, one of which is illustrated here. Cornices, molding or bamboo blinds can cover the lamps. A novel material for covering trays and side lamps is split wood. Cut thin strips to size and fasten them to shelves. Applying the same principle, many other materials could be used in this manner. (*Photograph by Gottscho-Schleisner*)

Any cabinet with shelves that would ordinarily hold books or bric-a-brac can be used as an indoor garden, as this photograph illustrates, with the simple addition of fluorescent lamps. (*Photograph courtesy of Verilux TruBloom*)

even shade-loving plants to grow: room dividers, bookshelves, china cabinets, recreation rooms, entrances, hallways. Obviously, the usual culture factors still apply: drafts and too-high or too-low temperatures are not good for plants growing under any conditions, whether artificial or natural.

What kind of plants can you grow? Any of the popular foliage plants. While most do well in natural shady locations, they will respond dramatically to the extra light and send forth lush new growth. Also, ferns, ivies, begonias, geraniums, African violets, palms and most hanging basket plants.

What kind of fixtures do you need? Most of the carts available commercially are not attractive enough for use in living rooms. They're meant to be placed out of sight, where plants are grown for the sake of growing them and not for showing them off. Of course, if you have space in the basement or have an extra-large kitchen, this could be your garden supply center, where on a rotating basis you bring plants to their flowering peak for displays in other parts of the house, later to be returned to their "nursery" when they begin to fade. But the real contribution of artificial lights to interior decoration lies in the growing of plants where they are to remain permanently, to be enjoyed twelve months a year.

Either fluorescent or incandescent lamps may be used. Fluorescent is preferred, and it's generally agreed that using both together produces the best results. If fluorescent lights are used alone, one tube should be the daylight type and the other cool white. Tubes come in many lengths, so that one can custom-design the area to be lighted. Tubes should be side-by-side—not end-to-end. There are also square and round fluorescent lamps (used in kitchens and basements) allowing the gardener greater variety in his designs.

Buy your fixtures at an electrical supply house or by mail from a specialty firm, so that you will be assured of getting safe equipment (tubes, metal frame, connectors and built-in ballast to regulate power input). White porcelain-coated or aluminum reflectors are used whenever possible to direct the light into the plants. Reflectors can be hidden from view by strips of molding when tubes are attached to shelves.

When combining fluorescent with incandescent lamps, use a ratio of about two to one in wattage—such as 50 watts of incandescent for every 100 of fluorescent.

Replace fluorescent tubes after 8,000 hours of burning, as their efficiency is greatly reduced by then.

When several baskets are hanging at different heights in a dark window, fluorescent tubes can be mounted vertically, hidden behind draperies. This principle is also effective for glass shelves in windows which face a wall and receive practically no light. Caution should be exercised, however, when it comes to placing tubes too near any flammable material.

Select a fluorescent fixture which is large enough to cover the plant area.

A fieldstone wall forms an attractive background for an indoor foyer garden. However, the incandescent lamps shown here are not sufficient for healthy plant growth. The ceiling should be lowered and fluorescent lamps installed. To keep the highlights of the textured wall, a single row of tiny R30 reflector incandescent lamps could be used along with the fluorescents. This done, decoration and horticulture would be successfully merged. (*General Electric Company photograph*)

There's no need to skip hanging baskets if light is insufficient. Ceramic cylinders and globes hold 75-watt Vita-Lite plant lamps which shine directly on basket planters. (Note to do-it-yourself fans: try large, perforated metal cans, sprayed a flat black.) Wall-mounted spotlights have adjustable angles; they come with cord, plug and switch. Use two of these, criss-crossing their beams on a floor plant. (*Photograph courtesy of Fleco Industries, Dallas, Texas*)

Since fixtures come in sizes that hold one, two, three or four tubes of varying lengths, there should be no problem in selecting the appropriate style. There are even "Midget" fixtures that are most useful for narrow shelves.

Incandescent bulbs may also be used alone for indoor gardening, but they give less light and greater heat per watt than do fluorescent tubes, which accounts for the greater popularity of the latter. However, there are times when a bulb hidden inside an attractive dome is the only decorative solution to lighting a plant in a room. Incandescent bulbs with their own built-in reflectors are preferable to the standard models because they stay bright longer, do not accumulate dirt and require less cleaning. It's imperative that all fixtures, whether fluorescent or incandescent, be kept clean of dust and dirt for maximum efficiency. Various types of dome reflectors are available for use with standard bulbs. Incandescent bulbs should be replaced after about 500 hours of use.

When it comes to large specimen plants, such as trees, mercury-vapor lamps are most effective. They are powerful enough to light, from a distance, an area that is several feet square. Check your electrical system in advance to make sure it will take these high-powered lamps, which need porcelain sockets. They can be fitted into goodlooking fixtures, which are then mounted on the wall or ceiling and aimed at the floor garden. At least two of these fixtures are necessary to floodlight the area thoroughly, their beams criss-crossing to cover the most ground. This type of lamp will keep plants with low light needs happy, but don't expect active growth.

Aware of the rapidly growing interest in indoor gardens, major lamp manufacturers have come out with many kinds of special "plant growth" lamps, both fluorescent and incandescent. Some are more efficient than others and should be carefully investigated before buying. These special lamps are not favored by experts in gardening under artificial lights, who prefer the combination of ordinary tubes and bulbs. I recommend keeping an open mind, trying out different lamps, noting results of plant growth carefully, and then sticking with what works best. New products come on the market every day,

Contemporary homes are especially suitable for dramatic lighting installations such as the one pictured here. The garden not only "furnishes" much of the living room, but acts as divider from other areas of the house. Ample fluorescent light is given the plants to prevent them from becoming tall and spindly. While such installations are admittedly costly, those who plan to build or remodel will find that the expense is not nearly so much as many other projects in the home, yet provides a permanent, striking indoor garden. (*General Electric Company photograph*)

after years of research spent on them, and one should not dismiss them without a fair trial. "TruBloom" lamps as of this date are considered among the best. But should you think that a sunlamp would be good for your plants, forget it. It provides ultraviolet rays for skin-tanning purposes which are detrimental to plant growth.

How much light should plants get? This depends on the plant, which is why it's a good idea to group together those requiring the same amount. Light intensity is measured by footcandles, and an inexpensive light meter can be purchased to eliminate guesswork.

A good rule of thumb is to follow the natural requirements of a plant. If it's sun-loving, requiring a great deal of light, its needs will be just the same under artificial lights. Miracles should not be expected from artificial lights—they cannot do everything that nature is able to do outdoors. But many plants do so well in this controlled indoor situation that we can, if we choose, have a lovely garden in our home all year long.

Plants vary from a minimum light requirement of 10 footcandles to a maximum of about 10,000. During the winter months, our homes vary from 10 to 1,000 footcandles. However, light meters measure the light as seen by the human eye, and the eye is not sensitive to the red and blue rays which are most important for plant growth. A scientific study of the various types of light rays is not necessary for the gardener who is interested only in growing plants for the decoration of his home. General guidelines are sufficient, and nothing replaces actual experience, as the experts agree when analyzing their own experiments. Perhaps this accounts for the differences of opinion about which is the best way of growing plants under artificial lights. We gardeners, whether of the outdoor or indoor variety, tend to be opinionated people who cling to our own theories with tenacity! I go by results. If a plant thrives, I feel that whatever it is that I'm doing must be right and I don't do a thing to change it.

The closer you place a plant to the lights, the greater will be the light intensity, and the same applies to a plant in relation to the center of the fixture. The highest intensity is directly under the middle of the lights, while on the edges there will be a drop in intensity. This is good to know so that you can put those plants which require less light under the far sides of the fixture. Another way of increasing light intensity is obvious: increase the number and/or the size of the lamps. This illustrates the importance of correct placement of the plant under the lights: when placed under the center of two 40-watt fluorescent tubes, a plant six inches from the lights receives 860 footcandles; if twelves inches away, it gets 500; and if eighteen inches away, it receives 380.

A difference should be noted between maintaining a plant and growing it. Most plants with low light requirements will maintain a status quo under

This room divider and planter, all in one, is an attractive wood-grained, stainless steel tubing unit with the fluorescent lamps carefully hidden from view. The illuminated translucent top allows display of glassware, or a regular shelf could be substituted to hold low-light plants. (*General Electric Company photograph*)

From the point of view of growing plants, portable lighted carts answer every need—but not so from the decor angle. They're best utilized in the kitchen or basement where they can serve as a home "nursery," propagating plants, rotating those in the house which are not looking their best, coddling young plants until they're mature enough to be displayed. Where space permits, these carts can be useful helpers to the indoor gardener. (*General Electric Company photograph*)

minimum light, but they will do much better and actively *grow* if placed in brighter light. The Department of Agriculture groups plants into four light categories: low, medium, high and very high, with the following descriptions:

Low is a minimum light level of 25 footcandles, but with 75 to 200 preferred. *Medium* is a minimum of 75 to 100, but with 200 to 500 preferred. *High* is a minimum of 200, but 500 is preferred. *Very high* is a minimum of 1,000 with over that amount preferred. Plants will grow well in a higher light level than is needed, but will definitely not survive *below* the minimum.

Much is made by hobbyists concerning the exact length of time that lights should be left on. When it comes to the majority of house plants, this need not worry the gardener. Most plants in this category are not fussy as to the length of day or night. Turn the lights on when you wake up and turn them off when you go to bed. Or, if you're afraid you might forget, buy a timer and set it for the hours required by the plants. Since you will have wisely grouped them according to similar light needs, a timer is a big help. But if you want fixtures in more than one room, or in several areas of a room, it's best to get into the habit of turning the lights on early in the morning and off at bedtime. It eventually becomes as routine as brushing your teeth. If you go away for a weekend, nothing horrible will happen to the plants if you don't turn on the lights, but this is not to be done frequently.

The culture of plants under artificial lights is the same as that under normal conditions. After all, you're merely attempting to duplicate the sun in an indoor environment. Light will never be as intense as it can get outdoors, but on the plus side, you are shielding your plants from such hazards as sudden downpours, windstorms, severe temperature changes and roaming animals.

Follow the same grooming, watering and fertilizing routine for house plants under artificial lights that you do for your other house plants. The only factor to watch out for is the intensity of light the plant is receiving when you first set it under the lights. If the stems are getting too tall, the plant is too far away from the lights; if its leaves curl under, it's too close. This is true of plants under natural light as well, but it's more pronounced under artificial conditions. By placing the plant on an inverted clay pot, you will bring it closer to the source of light, and by raising the lamp fixture, you will do the opposite. Experiment a bit for the first few weeks, and then relax and let the plants take over.

There should be a drop of 10 degrees or thereabouts from day to night temperatures, but this is usually the case in most homes anyway.

Light needs of plants. Most plants fit into the twelve- to sixteen-hour light cycle, with eighteen hours the maximum, but even cacti grow well under high light intensity for fourteen to sixteen hours a day. The following plants are some of the most popular and most likely to be grown indoors for decorative purposes. The information is taken from the U.S. Department of Agriculture's pamphlet on indoor gardens.

Name	*Light Need*
Aglaonema (Chinese evergreen)	low
Araucaria excelsa (Norfolk Island pine)	high
Asparagus sprengeri (asparagus fern)	medium
Begonias (other than rex)	very high
Bromeliads	medium
Chamaedorea elegans (Neanthe Bella palm)	low
Chamaedorea erumpens (bamboo palm)	low
Cissus antarctica (kangaroo vine)	high
Cissus rhombifolia (grape ivy)	medium
Codiaeum (croton)	very high
Coleus	very high
Dieffenbachia picta (dumbcane)	medium
Dizygotheca elegantissima (spider aralia)	high
Dracaena	medium
Fatsia japonica (aralia)	medium
Ficus	medium
Howea forsteriana (Kentia palm)	low
Hoya carnosa (wax plant)	medium
Maranta leuconeura (prayer plant)	medium
Nephrolepis exaltata bostoniensis (Boston fern)	medium
Pelargonium (geranium)	very high
Peperomia	low
Philodendrons	medium
Podocarpus	high
Saintpaulia (African violets)	very high
Spathiphyllum	medium

It should again be stressed that sunlight is much stronger than artificial light, which explains why some plants might be listed under "low" light needs for natural light situations indoors, but under "medium" needs when grown under artificial lights.

Plants can grow within six inches of a fluorescent lamp without any damage to the foliage. Incandescent bulbs without built-in reflectors release a tremendous amount of heat, which can cook plants placed too close. A clear shield of plastic or Plexiglas a couple of inches below the bulb screens out much of the heat, but it's easier to use several low-wattage bulbs instead of one or two strong ones. This spreads the heat over a larger area in a less intense way. The best bet is to buy bulbs with built-in reflectors and not worry about excessive heat. These cool-beam bulbs are well worth the small extra cost.

Terrariums, Miniature Gardens and Water Gardens

The easiest ways of decorating with plants and of bringing greenery into the home are with terrariums and miniature gardens. The former are made to order for people who travel a great deal or who simply won't be bothered with caring for plants on a regular basis.

TERRARIUMS

A terrarium is a world in complete control of its own atmosphere and needs. Strictly speaking, a terrarium is any clear glass container with a tightly-fitted glass cover and no opening whatsoever. Lucite and Plexiglas are good substitutes for glass. Light must be allowed to shine through the terrarium, which is why tinted glass should not be used. A tightly fitted lid is needed to keep the warm and humid atmosphere *inside* the terrarium, duplicating an environment similar to that of a greenhouse.

There is no limit to the number of shapes, sizes and styles of containers available for use as terrariums. Some are made with this use specifically in mind; others are simply a matter of using one's imagination as to their potential.

Since we are interested primarily in the use of terrariums as a significant factor in interior decoration, certain types of containers can be ruled out. Not

This is an effective way of making a terrarium the focal point of an indoor garden. A Plexiglas container and stand do not distract the eye from the plants. (*Cube terrarium, a do-it-yourself project of Plexiglas, Rohm and Haas Company*)

much of an impact on a room is made with a small marmalade jar holding one tiny plant. The larger the container, the more important the "statement" it will make in the room, as well as being easier to plant. It's also more fun because variety can be introduced in the miniature landscape. Broad-based containers hold many more plants than do tall narrow jars, and they allow your entire hand to get inside. Leave the large bottles with narrow necks to those who have already made several terrariums and who do it as a regular hobby. It takes skill to plant in a bottle, and a great deal of time and patience (and many failures). When you get right down to it, it's often done because it's freakish, and people will ask "How did you ever get those plants inside?" the way they inquire about the ship inside a bottle. For those interested in plants as well as decor, a square container is the best, or else a large acrylic plastic "bubble." The ideal terrarium is an old fish tank, not a new idea but still the best. Its size makes it possible to have an interesting landscape and a variety of plants.

If you have a handsome container, but it has no lid, it's an easy matter to

Coffee tables, even dining tables, are available with Plexiglas bowls which turn them into stunning terrariums. Care must be taken not to keep many objects on the top which would cut off light. (*Photograph courtesy of Dome Enterprises, Inc., Marathon, Florida*)

Here are some of the many shapes and sizes that are available in terrariums. Those that are bubble-shaped can also be suspended in hangers. Every day new styles appear on the market, but the simpler, classic lines are better for both the plants and the design of the room. (*Two photographs at left courtesy of Christen, Inc.; others courtesy of A.L. Randall Company; Plexiglas; and Rickes Crisa*)

have a glazier make one for you inexpensively. A fitted cover is functional as well as decorative. It's true that you could seal your terrarium with a strip of Saran Wrap—the results would be the same, but not so the esthetic effect.

The only way small terrariums can have an impact on a room is by borrowing the trick that works with plants in general: group several together. Plant three or four wide-mouthed glass containers of varying sizes, each one with different plants. Placed attractively on a table, these terrariums can create a handsome design that is important enough to be a focal point on its own.

The very first thing to do after you have selected the container is to make certain that it is absolutely clean. Scrub it in hot soap and water to which some household bleach has been added. Rinse thoroughly and allow it to dry naturally. If it's an old container, repeat this procedure several times. If the container is of glass and has a very wide mouth, put it through the dishwasher a few times, then rinse separately with bleach. The idea is to kill any bacteria that may be in the container.

Assemble on a table all the materials that you will need to make the terrarium: container, drainage material, charcoal, soil, plants, ornaments if any, water and tools.

Tools. You will need very few tools because your container, as we've already mentioned, has an opening wide enough for your hand to slip through. To make the holes into which you'll put the plants, you can buy a ¼-inch dowel at your local hardware store, or use a fat crayon or pen. Chopsticks are good for smaller holes. A very soft brush, such as used in applying eye shadow or painting watercolors, is good to dust the leaves after you're finished planting. Add a cork to the end of a chopstick for use as a tool for firming the soil, and use a small pickle fork as a rake. A pair of regular tweezers is excellent to pick up dead or broken-off leaves and a tiny manicure scissors is perfect for pruning. A bulb-shaped sprayer is a good way to water your terrarium, as you want a fine mist and not any harsh flow that would dislodge and harm the fragile plants.

Drainage Material. Since appearance is important in our decorating scheme, the best-looking drainage material is gravel. That's if the drainage layer shows (more of that later). Gravel may be bought in pet shops or garden supply centers. Rinse it several times in hot water and let it dry thoroughly.

Charcoal. You can buy small bags of charcoal already crushed, or else take a few lumps of ordinary barbecue charcoal and hammer them to little pieces.

Soil. It's definitely best to buy prepared, packaged potting soil which has already been sterilized for you. No need to bring in all kinds of bugs and weeds found in outdoor soil, or have to go through the sterilizing process yourself, which is a messy, unpleasant job in the oven. (Baking any soil creates a most unpleasant odor in the house.)

Here's a clever way of getting around having to get a plant into a bottle through its neck opening, saving hours of frustrating labor. (*Photograph courtesy of Rickes Crisa*)

A good soil mixture which is airy enough to allow proper drainage (important in a terrarium which has no drainage holes) is 2 parts of packaged soil mixture and one part of Perlite. No fertilizers have to be added because you don't want plants to grow to any great height. The idea is to keep them healthy, but not to push them into active growth. Later on—much later—when the plants have used up most of the nutrients in the soil, a water-soluble fertilizer can be added sparingly. For woodland plants, add one part of peat moss or humus to the soil mix described above.

Plants. Your selection of plant material depends chiefly on two factors: humidity and light. In a closed container, humidity is very high, and only plants which like this atmosphere will do well. Plants having similar cultural

Whether used as an end table with a Plexiglas terrarium or to show off two terrariums in the same space, these tables function as pieces of sculpture, striking accents in any decor. Have shade-loving plants at the bottom and those requiring more light on top. (*Photograph courtesy of Dome Enterprises, Inc., Marathon, Florida*)

requirements should be grouped in the same container. Humidity can be controlled to some degree by opening the terrarium periodically, but this is tricky. If the lid is left off for too long, the humidity may drop to a dangerously low level and be most detrimental to the plants. It's far better to select plants which thrive in high humidity in the first place. There are enough of them to provide a good selection.

Where you place the terrarium determines the amount of light it receives. No terrarium should ever be in direct sunlight, for the glass intensifies the heat and cooks the plants within. Indirect light is best, but there are degrees of this, as we all know. Some rooms are brighter than others.

Next to humidity and light, consider the size and shape of the container when choosing plants. Proportion is vitally important. A lot of tiny plants in a large fish tank are dull-looking and not worthy of a second look. Similarly, a tall plant completely filling a small container is ridiculous. In an attractive terrarium there must be some empty space, as there is in nature, with tall and low plants all tied together with a groundcover.

To save your temper as well as your time, try several groupings of plants on a newspaper, next to the container. Try to visualize the plants in the con-

Cacti and succulents surround a piece of Featherock and even grow out of its holes. Two or three of these on a sunny window sill form a handsome arrangement. Use miniature ferns and other dwarf foliage plants for a shadier spot. (*Photograph by Brian Manning*)

tainer. Fiddle around with the plants until you have a pleasing design. Keep in mind that if your terrarium is going to be seen from all sides, the design you create must be attractive all around.

Ornaments. Go easy on these. Don't include anything that nature herself wouldn't have—and she wouldn't have plastic villages scattered around. Keep ornaments natural-looking and unobtrusive. Tiny bits of driftwood simulate fallen logs in a woodland setting. Boulders are easily made out of Featherock (lightweight volcanic rock from the High Sierra country of California, avail-

The squat strawberry jar, a good choice for informal rooms, lends itself to upright and trailing plants. Stuff moss around plants coming out of holes to prevent soil from washing out during watering. (*Photograph by Brian Manning*)

The author's smallest indoor garden! A hairy cactus grows happily out of a shell. Nature's own creations—driftwood, shells, logs—make unusual containers. (*Photograph by Brian Manning*)

able from mail order houses—see pages 226-232—or at some of the better garden supply centers). A stream can be outlined by fine sand. For a pond, it's more natural to use a broken bit of dark mirror instead of ordinary mirror, which looks artificial, and edge it with moss.

Planting. Now that you have gathered the materials, and you have a basic idea of the design you want to achieve, we can proceed with the actual planting.

1. Preferring the most naturalistic results possible, I don't like to see the various layers of drainage, charcoal, and soil showing through the glass. If you feel the same way, line the sides of the terrarium with green moss, the moss side facing out. If you're hanging your terrarium, line the bottom as well. (Small bags of green sheet moss are available in florists' and garden supply stores.) It's easier to apply if you moisten the moss first. Put it into a pan of water and squeeze the water out thoroughly. The moss will then stay flat and in place when you put it against the glass.

2. Drainage material is next. A good rule of thumb is that the entire planting mixture should be about a fourth of the depth of the terrarium, drainage layer included. More than two inches of drainage is not necessary, however, so stop there, no matter how much soil you put on top of it. A one-inch layer of gravel is the norm for a twelve-inch-high terrarium. Spread the gravel evenly at the bottom of the container.

3. Cover the drainage material with a layer of charcoal. If you're not using the moss liner, pour charcoal very slowly and carefully, as the dust will coat the inside of the glass walls and create an unsightly mess that you'll have to clean up. Charcoal is used to keep the soil pure and sweet since the container has no holes to allow excess water to drain out.

4. In order to prevent the soil from seeping into the drainage material, which should be kept free and porous to do a proper job, it's a good idea to spread a very thin layer of sheet moss over the charcoal. A friend of mine swears by her old nylon pantyhose—she simply cuts a piece and spreads it over the charcoal. Discarded coffee filters are also good.

Next, pour the soil mixture evenly into the container, creating several levels or mounds as your landscaping plan dictates. Obviously, the size of the terrarium plays an important role here. Only in the largest containers will you be able to have an intricate landscape. In others, you can create terrain interest with the soil level higher on one side, dipping into a "valley." Use a funnel to pour the soil inside the container. With a spoon, move the soil around and try different surface levels. Don't attempt several tiny designs in one container. Plants will quickly grow over these, and you'll lose the whole effect. One bold design is far easier to achieve. You should now have one-fourth of the container filled.

5. The actual planting. Start with the larger plants, since they will need the biggest holes. Don't hesitate to change your mind and move them around, if your earlier "dry run" on the newspaper doesn't come out quite the way you visualized. All the plants will grow some, so allow room accordingly. Remove plants very gently from their pots and carefuly shake off excess soil, leaving the root ball intact. Put the plant at the same soil level it was in the pot. You can tell this by the soil mark on the stem of the plant. Whatever depth it was inside the original pot, that's the depth it needs to be planted in the terrarium.

Don't put plants too close together. In a few months they'll fill in the gaps and will be all the healthier for the extra room you allowed them. When all the plants are in, firm the soil and rake it smooth. (Use that cork-tipped stick or the back of a tablespoon for firming, and a fork for raking.)

Now put in your ground cover, which can be plants or green moss. Ground cover plants quickly take over, so be sparing. I used baby's-tears in one terrarium—a bit too generously—and it grew so rapidly and thickly that it threatened to take over the whole landscape. I had to carefully dig some up, but this nearly damaged nearby plants, so that now I have to keep pruning it back. Avoid such a mistake by being overly cautious. It's easier to add more ground covers later on, if you still have bare spots, than it is to take them out.

If you lined the terrarium with moss, now is the time to trim it if it shows above the soil line. If only a bit peeps out, it's easy to push it under the soil, but if much shows, use a pair of scissors to cut it off.

6. Water the entire terrarium slowly and carefully. Use a sprayer or a small paper cup with its rim bent to create a trickle when the water pours out. Watch out for overwatering. Most terrariums fail because plants rot in too much water. Unlike potted houseplants, which should be watered thoroughly until the water comes out the bottom, no such thing should be done to a terrarium because of its lack of drainage holes. To test whether you've watered your newly planted terrarium adequately, do the trusted finger test: stick your finger into the soil, about one inch deep. If the soil is damp, that's enough watering. If it's dry, keep adding water slowly until it's moist to the one-inch depth. Of course, if you don't use the moss liner, simply watch the water make its way downward and you'll know when to stop.

Use a soft brush to clean leaves which may have some soil on them, and then mist all the foliage. Put the lid back on top of the terrarium and you're finished!

Planting a terrarium is fun because it allows your creative ability to show itself. You can follow directions step-by-step concerning the mechanics of planting but no one can, or should, tell you how to arrange the plants. There

Simple steps in planting a terrarium.

OPPOSITE ABOVE: Assemble all materials needed: container, plants, gravel, soil, charcoal bits and decorative green sheet moss (if needed to line container below soil level). Tools are unnecessary when a removable cover permits easy access to the plants. OPPOSITE, BELOW: Put gravel at bottom of container with charcoal bits mixed in lightly, then add soil. Start with the tallest plants, ending with ground cover plants (those that creep on the surface of soil). Water it thoroughly and replace the airtight cover. ABOVE: The finished terrarium. (*Photographs by Brian Manning*) are many plants to choose from, and as many ways of displaying them. No two terrariums can ever be the same, even when planted by one person, which might explain the popularity of this form of gardening.

Don't believe that once your terrarium is finished, you should never touch it again. This is a form of gardening like any other, only done in miniature, and there is no reason why you can't rectify a mistake if it annoys you, or introduce a pretty new plant just given to you which is ideally suited to terrarium culture. You'll derive far greater satisfaction if you follow your terrarium's growth closely and participate actively in its changes.

Maintenance. A closed terrarium is easy to maintain because it controls its atmosphere and attends to its own needs. Its temperature is not affected by that of the room since the container is sealed off from the outside. The humidity level is similarly kept even, building up periodically to create "rain" that temporarily fogs the inside of the container. The water goes back into the soil and is then absorbed by the plant's root system, only to be given off again by the leaves, repeating the whole cycle.

Drafts are nonexistent, and bugs can't get in (that's why you have to be careful not to introduce them or any disease with the original planting). Once a month, check the soil to see if it needs watering. Again, do the trusted finger test. If the soil feels moist, leave it alone. If it's dry to about one inch below the surface, add water sparingly. If fogging on the inside of the glass or plastic persists for more than one day, open the lid for a few hours until it clears up. Fogging is natural but shouldn't continue for any real length of time. Condensation shows that the "rain" cycle is working properly. Watering with a spray bulb is good, as it not only gives water to the soil but also refreshes the foliage and re-establishes the humidity pattern.

It cannot be overemphasized that you should rely on the finger test for watering needs. Even if plants look somewhat sick, don't assume it's from lack of water unless your finger tells you so. There could be other reasons, such as too strong a light. Bright light is good, but direct sunlight is definitely not. My terrarium is a good six feet from the nearest window, in a bright room, but never in full sun. In the summer, I draw the window shades during the middle of the day to prevent the stronger sun rays from reaching it. I turn it periodically since, of course, the plants lean toward the side that has the most light. Obviously, you can't do that with a heavy fish tank. The only way to beat this leaning Tower of Pisa syndrome is to install a row of artificial lights in back and above the tank to compensate for the natural light hitting the front.

Grooming a terrarium is based on the same principles that apply for any other indoor garden. Pick up dead leaves and decayed material. Prune back plants which are outgrowing the container and which you wish to keep in check. The manicure scissors mentioned earlier are excellent for this. If a plant is dead or looks diseased, pull it out and replace it with a new one. If you find that you persistently lose the same type of plant, it's no doubt because it's not suitable for a terrarium in the first place.

It's best to skip fertilizing altogether unless you strictly adhere to a very weak solution (diluted to one-fourth of the manufacturer's instructions) and fertilize only about twice a year. Besides not wanting the plants to grow rapidly, the other reason for little fertilizing is that the excessive fertilizer salt build-up has no way of draining out of the container.

If you place the terrarium in a dark corner of the room, you will need artificial lighting to keep it healthy. Stick with plants that have low light needs and follow the same guidelines that would apply for houseplants under artificial lights (see previous chapter). Fluorescent lights are best, placed from 8 to 16 inches above the foliage. Experiment a bit by moving the lamp up and down, observing the reaction of the plants. If they grow too leggy, they need more light. If they're all cramped together, looking as if they are trying to shield themselves from too much light, that's precisely what they're trying to do, so place the lamp farther away. The powerful mercury vapor lights (see page 85) are an excellent way to spotlight a terrarium from a distance of several feet. As with other plants grown under artificial lights, the lamp should be turned off at night to give the plants a chance to rest, and turned on when you wake up in the morning. Get into the habit of doing this, or else buy a timer.

Because a terrarium is sealed off from the rest of the world, pests and diseases are rarely a problem. However, no matter how carefully you examined each plant before planting it, and no matter how wise your use of sterilized soil, there still might have been some dormant element which appears later on. The all-purpose insecticide spray that you use on houseplants can be used on the terrarium, if you have no ferns. (Ferns are damaged by sprays.) Spray the plants carefully, wipe off any liquid from the inside of the glass and the cover, and close the lid to allow the fumes to do their job. Open briefly an hour later to let any excess fumes out, and then close the terrarium. Systemic insecticides, which are applied to the soil either in solid or liquid form, are excellent, as they can be used with any plants, ferns included. Always follow the manufacturer's directions carefully. This is most important.

The most common insects that you may find on your plants are aphids, mealybugs, scale, spider mites, thrips and white flies (see pages 218-219). Unlike a potted plant, the infected plant can't be taken to the kitchen sink to be washed with soap and water. But you can try washing its leaves with a Q-Tip dipped in a soapy solution, or in alcohol in the case of mealybugs.

The usual disease found inside a terrarium is mold, which is a type of fungus. Unless the plant is suited to the high humidity of a closed terrarium, it will develop a mold and rot, sometimes infecting plants nearby. Quickly remove any plant that is in this condition. Other reasons could be that it had the mold before you planted it, or that you have simply overwatered the plants. After you have removed the infected plants, play safe and dust the remaining ones with a fungicide. Watch your watering carefully—keep it on the dry side for a while—and remove the lid for a couple of hours if you see excessive fogging. Don't let foliage touch the sides of the glass, as this induces rot.

A note of caution to those wishing to introduce some small animals, such as baby turtles, into a terrarium. Don't. It's not fair to the animals who must have live food or will eagerly eat up the plants around them. They create havoc with your carefully planned landscape. Pets are a separate hobby from gardening, and deserve special attention to their particular needs in an ecologically-sound environment for *them*—not for the plants.

MINIATURE GARDENS

A miniature garden is a grouping of small plants in an open container. If a terrarium has an open hole at the top, strictly speaking, it's a miniature garden because it's not in control of its own atmosphere. Containers for these are plentiful: large brandy snifters, clay saucers, clay animals, squat strawberry jars, bonsai pots, clear plastic containers, ceramic bowls. These come in all shapes, colors and sizes, but simplicity is best. The container selected for a miniature landscape is important to the overall appearance of the garden, and clean lines and unobtrusive colors will not detract from the plants.

As with small terrariums, *dish gardens* do not contribute an important accent to a room. By itself, in a corner of a table, a small dish with plants is easily overlooked. If only one is displayed, it should be a fairly large one—roughly the size of a dinner plate, as opposed to a teacup—and placed in a spot that can't help but catch one's attention. I have two miniature gardens, one in a low strawberry jar and the other in a saucer that is normally used for a large clay pot, and have grouped them on a window sill with a few potted plants, also in clay pots. The similarity in the containers unifies the entire grouping. Were the containers to be scattered around the room, the impact would be totally lost.

A bit of whimsy can be introduced in miniature gardens with the use of clay animals as pots for herbs, grouped on a kitchen window sill. As with containers for potted plants, stay away from the cute, overly decorated designs. Don't overlook nature herself when it comes to unusual containers. Large shells, pieces of driftwood and hollowed Featherock all make attractive containers.

The biggest drawback to this type of gardening is that the container has no drainage holes and utmost care must be exercised in watering the plants. If you use a container that does have drainage holes, place it on a matching saucer. Clay is porous, so that even if a saucer is used, it can still damage the table top with excessive dampness seeping through. Line the saucer with foil.

Because they're both in waterproof containers, miniature gardens are planted in the same way as terrariums. The dish should be at least four inches deep to allow room for the roots to develop adequately. A layer of drainage material is first spread at the bottom; then the charcoal, and then the soil. See pages 209-210 for soil mixes, choosing the one that is suitable for the plants selected. Mixture #1 (all-purpose soil) is good for most plants, mixture #2 for acid-loving plants and mixture #3 for cacti and succulents. Only plants requiring similar soil should be planted together in the same dish.

Unlike that of a closed terrarium, the atmosphere of the miniature garden in an open or partially open container is entirely your responsibility. Excessive heat or cold, drafts, watering, humidity are all up to you to prevent or supply. These gardens need precisely the same care and attention that you give to your potted plants. After all, a miniature garden is several plants in one pot, so that there is no difference, except for watering. It is better to not water enough than to gamble on overdoing it, for excess water will collect at the bottom, rotting the roots eventually. The finger test for soil moisture is more crucial than ever in this type of gardening. Use a paper cup to trickle water slowly and sparingly. Cacti and succulents should never be misted from above, as they dislike humidity, and soil should be allowed to go absolutely dry before you water again.

Which plants to select? It depends on your taste and the shape of your container. A large brandy snifter holds in greater moisture and humidity than does a shallow dish, making it more appropriate for certain plants. Only miniature plants or seedlings are used in a garden of this type. Too often one sees, in florists' windows, open containers filled to the rim with plants that will quickly grow far too large for them. The average house plant is not suitable, unless it's a dwarf variety—and since plants today come in so many sizes and varieties, the choice is far from meager. A walk through nearby woods will reveal all kinds of tiny plants, growing through moss, that will take a long time to grow to any height. Many are seedlings of trees—but no need to worry that they will reach forest size soon!

The rich variety of cacti and succulents available and their generally slow-growing habits make them ideal for dish gardens in a sunny spot. Combine varieties that sprawl over the edge of the container with others that are skinny and tall and fat and squat. Unify the design with a few handsome stones or a piece of Featherock, with a cavity or two hollowed out for more plants. Cover the soil surface with fine gravel or smooth pebbles (some beautiful ones are sold in oriental shops). If the container is large enough, you

can create a landscape with two levels of soil forming a slope or hill. Have a pine seedling as the "tree."

Bonsai is an art, as anyone knows who has been fortunate enough to have seen fine Japanese examples. Essentially, bonsai is the dwarfing of trees that would be forest giants if left to grow naturally. By careful, patient shaping and pruning and restriction of the root growth, these trees remain miniatures. The gnarled shapes of the trunks and branches give this form of gardening its unique character. Botanical gardens have centuries-old specimens on display to provide inspiration to would-be hobbyists.

One need not be a purist strictly following bonsai principles and philosophy to produce some charming results. And the bonus is that some unorthodox bonsai plants can be enjoyed indoors, as opposed to the genuine

Superb specimens, one of which is over a century old, illustrate the beauty, grace and skill of bonsai. These pines would not survive indoors permanently, but other plants which are suitable for apartment culture can be similarly trained. (*Photographs courtesy of Brooklyn Botanic Garden*)

bonsai trees of temperate zone that must be kept outdoors all year in order to go through their natural dormant periods. The Japanese bring them in for special occasions, but this is not suitable for our purpose of growing and displaying plants on a permanent basis for interior decorating.

A collection of three bonsai plants, attractively grouped in a room, makes a striking indoor garden. It is an exotic form of landscaping that is a real attention-getter.

Selection of the container requires careful thought. Shape and scale are important. A plant with a spreading habit or long, horizontal branches needs a rectangular or oblong pot which follows the lines of the plant. A single, tree-like plant with an upright growth habit is best in a square or round pot. I prefer the classic, solid dark colors when it comes to containers. The dull-finish blacks, browns and grays are best for pottery, and the warmth of wood is a perfect foil for certain plants. Glazed pottery is not healthy for the plants, at least not when also glazed on the inside. Overly-decorated, pseudo-oriental containers are cheap imitations of the handsome originals, and distract the eye from the beauty of the plant.

All-purpose potting soil (mixture #1) is fine for most bonsai plants. The soil should be on the "poor" side anyway, since active growth is precisely what is not desired. As with terrariums and dish gardens, the aim is to keep the plants healthy, but not to encourage them to reach their full size.

The range of available plants for bonsai-like gardening is so wide that it's impossible to list them all. They must meet only two requirements: to be able to survive indoors year round and to have an interesting shape that lends itself to training and pruning. The "freaks" of nature that one quickly passes over at the local nursery are just the ones to look for. There are dwarf varieties of many plants now being developed and readily available. Tropical zone plants have no problems surviving indoors.

As scale is so important, look for plants with tiny leaves and odd-shaped stems as opposed to those that are straight as an arrow with no interesting twists and bends. It takes tremendous skill to take a perfect branch and slowly bend it to your own will, so if nature has started the job for you, take advantage of it. Use thin copper wire to keep the branches in place or to encourage a different shape; leave it on for several months at least. Proceed slowly when pruning leaves and bits of branches, keeping in mind that design you want to achieve. You may change your mind halfway through and try for something else, but that's the fun of it. Since you're not out to cultivate the traditional bonsai forms, you can allow yourself some flexibility.

Certain plants lend themselves better than others to bonsai culture. I had a *Carissa grandiflora* for several years, growing it as a regular house plant, until I realized one day that its slow growth, its fascinating branching habits and smallish leaves were perfect for training and pruning. I cut away some of the roots (which should be done with *all* plants that are to be "dwarfed"), repotted it in a totally different container, pruned it a bit, and presto, I had a bonsai plant!

Rosemary is not only a highly fragrant herb, but its shrub-like growing habit offers all sorts of possibilities for interesting designs. Small citrus trees are good, as are certain types of rex begonias, the low, hanging form of gardenia, and weeping fig. If you have a room in the house which is kept unusually cool in the winter, you can try pyracantha and *Buxus japonica* and *B. microphylla compacta*, two good forms of boxwood, as well as various types of dwarf Japanese junipers. Seedlings of trees, both deciduous and evergreen, while suitable, need the outdoor seasonal cycles to survive. Dwarf geraniums and those with old, woody stems also take well to training; you might also try podocarpus and any of the many small-leaved ivies.

For bonsai, use containers with drainage holes and matching saucers, and keep the plant evenly moist, waiting until the soil dries out a bit before rewatering. If roots grow out the bottom holes, cut them off. You may wish to go to one pot larger; if so, prune the roots before repotting, to further retard the growth of the plant. And skip fertilizing altogether.

SUGGESTED PLANTS FOR CLOSED TERRARIUMS

(stars indicate plants that also do well in an open container with sides)

Anthurium scherzerianum (flamingo flower)

Asparagus plumosus nanus (dwarf asparagus fern)

*Begonias—dwarf varieties

Caladium humboldtii

Calathea

**Chamaedorea elegans bella* (dwarf parlor palm)

Chamaeranthemum—varieties

Cissus antarctica minima (dwarf kangaroo ivy)

Cissus striata (dwarf grape ivy)

Dionaea muscipula (Venus flytrap)

**Episcia*—varieties

Euonymus fortunei minimus (Good ground cover for larger terrariums, as is *E. fortunei uncinatus*.)

*Ferns (Miniature varieties best for small containers.)

Ficus repens (or F. *pumila minima*) (Good for ground cover.)

Fittonia—varieties

**Hedera helix*—dwarf varieties (Good for ground cover.)

**Helxine soleirolii* (baby's-tears) (Dainty ground cover.)

**Impatiens*—dwarf varieties

**Malpighia coccigera* (dwarf holly)

Maranta—varieties

**Peperomia*—varieties

**Saxifraga sarmentosa* (strawberry begonia) (Creeps and forms new plants like strawberries.)

Selaginella (moss fern)—varieties (A good ground cover for larger terrariums. Use dwarf variety for smaller containers.)

**Spathiphyllum cannaefolim* (Only for use in large fish tanks when tall, lush green leaves are needed for background.)

SUGGESTED PLANTS FOR OPEN CONTAINERS

(In addition to those starred under "Closed Terrariums,")

Aglaonema—varieties

Buxus microphylla japonica (Japanese boxwood—dwarf variety)

Cacti and succulents—includes crassula, kalanchöe, sedum and sempervivum (Best for shallow containers and squat strawberry jars. Countless varieties to choose from. Give full sun.)

Ceropegia (rosary vine)—varieties

Dizygotheca elegantissima (false aralia) (Buy tiny plant, it grows slowly.)

Dracaena (Buy small plants only.)

Pelargonium (geranium) (Miniature varieties. Give full sun and a wide open container for good air circulation.)

Pilea—varieties

Podocarpus macrophyllus maki (shrubby yew pine) (Grows slowly and is easy to keep to desired height.)

Rosa (miniature roses) (Need high humidity but also good air circulation. Watch out for pests. Many varieties.)

Saintpaulia (African violet) (Miniature varieties best for medium-sized container.)

Scindapsus

Streptocarpus (cape primrose) (Will thrive wherever African violets do.)

Syngonium—varieties (Good for medium to large containers.)

NOTE: Use judgment when it comes to defining the amount of humidity and air circulation that an "open" container has. There is a vast difference between a shallow dish and a terrarium whose cover has a hole an inch or two in diameter. A brandy snifter falls in between. A rule of thumb is that the more humidity-loving a plant is, the smaller the opening of the container should be—the ultimate being the totally-sealed terrarium.

Plants are much more flexible, however, than we give them credit for. They can adapt nicely to different situations, and of course much depends, as discussed earlier in this chapter, on where you place the container. The degree of light it receives in the course of the day helps to determine the temperature inside the container, and the temperature inside the home as a whole also has an effect on the container. If you group plants of similar cultural requirements in the same container, you have only to experiment with the location of the container if plants look below par. The tiniest evidence of new growth tells you that the plant is happy.

And finally, a good source of plant material is the great outdoors. Your own backyard, a walk through the woods, the roadside, all will reveal plants suitable for miniature gardens. Seedlings of trees, while unsuited for indoor bonsai, are especially attractive for terrariums and dish gardens because you won't worry if some of these wild plants don't last long. They will have given you much joy in the meantime. For that matter, don't expect any indoor landscape to last indefinitely without need for replacements.

Wildflowers are very precious, so don't pull out plants at random. It's easy to say that you should check with your local agricultural county agent, or carry a book on wildflowers with the endangered species checked off, but this is not very practical for a beginner at this whole game. Instead, follow this procedure and you'll still qualify as a responsible, conservation-minded citizen: *only dig out a plant when you see quite a few of the same all around it.* You will be giving nature a chance to propagate the plants via all those you leave behind.

When digging a plant, take enough of the soil to keep the root ball fully covered, and put the entire plant inside a plastic bag with a few drops of water. Keep it in a cool place until you get home, and plant it immediately in your terrarium or dish garden. Mosses are great and besides, you never know what lies dormant inside. Months later, a tiny green plant emerges from the moss to create a charming miniature landscape. Never mind that you won't know its name; simply enjoy nature's surprise.

WATER GARDENS

You can call it hydroculture or hydroponics if you're in a fancy mood, but to me *water gardening* is a way of growing house plants so effortlessly that only the plastic variety could be more foolproof. No problem about under- or overwatering, no repotting, no soil mix worries, no guilt feelings during vacations with painful surprises awaiting your return. For anyone who has convinced himself (wrongly but persistently) that he is totally incapable of growing anything green in his house, water gardening is the answer. It demands so little care that I am ashamed to admit I keep forgetting I have several such "water gardens" in my home.

Virtually any plant will grow in water, but foliage ones are sensational. Use cuttings long enough to reach at least halfway down the container, or buy potted plants. If you use the latter, gently remove the plant from its pot and soak the roots in the kitchen sink until the soil is thoroughly loosened. Rinse away all traces of soil. Cut off any leaves that go below the surface of the water in the container.

Choose a waterproof container that goes well with the decor of the room where it is to be placed. Create a small garden by grouping a few containers together. It's a question of personal taste whether you prefer a clear container or not. If you're fascinated with watching roots grow, select clear glass; otherwise, anything will do. Cache-pots and jardinieres make wonderful containers. The only taboo is metal, but there is nothing to stop you from using that fabulous brass or copper urn if you first put the plants inside a glass container and then insert it in the urn. A wide container allows you to grow more plants and makes a greater "statement."

Locate the container with its plants exactly as you would any other house plant. If they're low-light plants, keep them out of direct sunlight; if medium, give bright light; if sun-loving, place in full sun. Avoid the last, however, if you use a clear glass container. Select an opaque pot if you're going to put the plants in a south window.

Whatever container you use should be absolutely clean. If it can take the dishwasher, run it through once, or twice if very dirty. A hot soapy solution, with household bleach added, cleans pots that can't be put in the washer.

Fill the container with water, adding some charcoal bits if you wish—some of mine have charcoal, others don't, and frankly I can't see any difference in the results. Sunlight is what encourages the growth of algae in the water, and since most plants grown indoors require low to medium light away from sun, algae isn't much of a problem. But clear glass containers are more prone to algae, since they allow light in.

All you need do next is put the plants in the container. If they fall over, anchor them with clean stones, pebbles, gravel or marbles. Whether you use only one type of plant or mix several in a container is up to you. Try both ways. Have one bowl filled only with a ruffled variety of ivy, and another mixing multicolored coleus with Chinese evergreen and one of the cut-leaf philodendrons. The combinations are endless, but in the same pot, it's best to have only one brilliantly-colored plant set off by one or more green ones.

If you suspend the water garden in a handsome rope hanger, plant wandering Jews, pothos, grape ivy or any other hanging plants. Don't be afraid to experiment. The worst that can happen is that it won't grow—but chances are that it will.

If plants get leggy or too large, prune them back. Add weak liquid fertilizer every few months, diluted to at least half the strength recommended by the manufacturer.

Caring for your water garden consists chiefly of maintaining the water level in the container and of washing everything out every so often. I know that it's recommended that this be done once a month, but I certainly never get around to doing it that often, and I can't complain about the results! However, it's a good idea to empty the container, wash it thoroughly, rinse all the plant roots, and put everything back into clean water, plus charcoal if you use it. If you make sure that dead leaves don't fall into the water, and that no live ones get below the water level, you'll avoid a big source of waste material that contributes to polluted water.

Don't overlook tree branches. I cut some pussywillows and put them in water. Roots developed, and long after the "pussies" had passed on to their next stage of development, the branches were still going strong. The same thing happens with forsythia. Leaves appear after the flowers are gone, and the branches live on happily. Those that don't "take" (not growing roots), I throw out, keeping the others that are merrily growing.

Vegetables–Herbs–Bulbs

Even back in our grandmothers' days, some vegetables and fruits were grown indoors as house plants, strictly for their foliage value. Who hasn't grown up with at least one sweet potato vine, or multiple attempts at getting the sliced top of the pineapple to root, or carrots' dainty foliage? And let's not overlook the forever-popular avocado, and planting the pits and seeds of black olives, grapefruits, oranges, lemons, etc. It was done for fun, and if it succeeded, fine; if not, there were always more on next week's dinner table for another try. A few pots of herbs on the kitchen window sill rounded out the picture of non-house plants around the house.

VEGETABLES

Today, two factors tempt us into growing vegetables indoors: the craving for truly fresh produce, which even when not-so-fresh has become terribly expensive, and the many new dwarf varieties of vegetables which have been introduced by the seed companies.

A few words of caution, however. Most vegetables are not pretty to see growing, so that from a decoration point of view, they are not, by and large, to be recommended. I know that ads speak glowingly of certain vegetables cascading from hanging baskets, while some fancy espalier work is done with others. It just won't work. Vegetables need room to grow, even the dwarf varieties, and as they have to be thinned out to make room for nice, plump specimens, you can imagine how many you would harvest even if every seed you planted grew.

It should be stressed at this point that I am referring strictly to window sill gardening, totally indoors. Growing vegetables on a city terrace or in a town backyard, while having the usual urban difficulties to cope with, is entirely different. The vegetables are grown outdoors in the soil or in half-bushel baskets, which are suitable containers for growing mini-varieties. But in this book we are only concerned with plants grown strictly for interior decoration purposes.

Even when looks are not a factor, growing vegetables on window sills presents a formidable challenge. While writing this book, I read in a New York newspaper an article about a woman who had grown a fantastic variety of vegetables in her city apartment. I immediately contacted her, excited at the prospect of getting information straight from someone who *did* it. This was in early winter, and I was all set to have a photographer follow each of her steps the following spring and summer, to record all of this for my readers.

The lady gardener had a large apartment with several exposures, as well as the use of her next-door neighbor's apartment, where she was allowed to utilize all the windowsills in the spirit of experimentation. All kinds of vegetables were planted. Hundreds of pounds of soil and fertilizer were tracked through the apartments. Redwood boxes were made to fit the window sills. The lady didn't care about looks, she wanted results. And these were disastrous considering the time, effort and money that had gone into the summer's venture. As seemingly easy a vegetable as pepper didn't produce. The cherry tomatoes did well in a south window. Herbs, radishes, chives and scallions also were good. Cool-weather crops such as lettuce and spinach can't take the city heat.

The space, of course, was insufficient to grow enough to feel rewarded for the work done. This lady had over a dozen window sills at her disposal, all put to duty, and she felt deeply disappointed. She told me that the following spring she would limit herself to a few tomatoes and herbs. For one thing, her husband had complained about the high cost of the soil and fertilizers.

For house dwellers who have a plant room or a porch, enclosed or not, half a dozen large tubs can form a small vegetable garden if the exposure is sunny enough. Obviously this is assuming that the backyard is so tiny that there is no room to plant vegetables directly into the soil, where they do best. Radishes, which take up relatively little room, can be planted all around the rim of a large tub, leaving room in the center for a cherry tomato. Tomatoes have very soft, fleshy stems, so when staking them, don't use twine or wire. Cut strips of soft cloth or worn pantyhose. (Don't laugh, they're super for this, and it makes up for the frustration of seeing that perfectly good left leg going to waste. With or without runs, give it a try.)

For apartment dwellers, let me say that it's best to forget growing your own vegetables, for decorative purposes or any other. If you want to try it strictly for fun and adventure, then go ahead. Should weight be a problem, synthetic soil is a good substitute for the regular kind; however, you must follow a rigid fertilizing schedule, since no fertilizer exists in the mixture. You can buy synthetic soil ready-made at most garden supply stores, or mix it yourself: 1 bushel vermiculite, 1 bushel shredded peat moss, 1¼ cups ground dolomite limestone, ½ cup of 20 percent superphosphate, 1 cup 5-10-5 fertilizer. Mix thoroughly.

For those with a terrace or a backyard garden, I suggest getting one of the good books or pamphlets on the subject (see the Bibliography on pages 234-236), so that you are properly armed. One person's failure can very well be another's success, so an open mind should be kept. The supposed ease and beauty of raising vegetables in the living room is more fancy than fact.

HERBS

Herbs are deservedly popular because they are attractive looking as well as not too hard to grow—not to mention delicious to eat in any number of dishes that would be dull without them. Always keeping in mind the decorative aspect of our form of indoor gardening, you can grow herbs in all kinds of handsome containers. Those fun clay animal planters described earlier are great for the kitchen or an enclosed porch, as long as they are large enough. Once past the seedling stage, herbs develop a good root system and need room. A three-inch pot is the barest minimum in size. Repot to the next size larger when roots start growing through the drainage hole.

Good containers are standard clay pots or some of the fancier adaptations. If possible, set the pots on a tray of pebbles on a window sill. Keep the pebbles (or gravel) moist, thereby adding humidity to the area surrounding the plants. While it's true that most herbs originated in the sunny climate of the Mediterranean, which is dry and hot, nothing approximates the lack of humidity in an apartment. Another suggestion, mentioned so often in this book, is double-potting. If you put a porous clay pot inside a waterproof container and fill the open space with peat moss (kept moist), the roots of the plants will never dry out and the humidity generated by the damp moss will keep the herbs happy. True, you've read that herbs like a dry spot—but what is considered dry in outdoor garden soil is a whole different story from your kitchen window sill in full sun.

Pot the herbs the way you would any house plant. First the drainage material, and then the soil. Soil mix #1—the all-purpose kind—is good (see page 209), but don't fertilize afterwards. Herbs have a more pungent aroma if kept underfed. Water when the soil dries out completely, and then water thoroughly.

A word of advice. Please avoid those pre-packaged herb kits. They're cute as can be, *but*—the pots are far too small, and although some of them are meant to hang, where does the drainage water go since there are no saucers attached? And, most important, some of the herbs are of the most difficult variety to grow from seed—indoors or out. Instead, buy pots of the right size (chives need a six-inch pot, for instance), and plants or seeds, and make your own soil mix.

My urgent recommendation is that you start with potted seedlings available at the local garden supply store. Believe me, simple as it may seem, herbs do not germinate that quickly. I am wild about dill, for instance, and grow it only with the greatest difficulty in my greenhouse, where it has ideal conditions. Most gardeners I know say the same thing: the indoor gardener who's a beginner at all this should get a few pots of already started plants and avoid a good deal of frustration. Dill, rosemary, thyme, mint and the popularly available chives (transplanted to a larger pot) are best bought already growing. Tarragon (make sure it's French tarragon, not the flavorless Russian variety) is another herb usually found already potted. Work backwards is my advice. First buy any herb that is already started for you, and then try your luck at starting others from seed.

Wait until the plant is pretty fully grown before snipping away at it, but afterwards, don't worry. Constant "pruning" keeps it bushy. When starting herbs from seed, double the sand or perlite in the soil mixture to make it lighter; fill the pot, sprinkling the seeds thinly and covering them with a very thin layer of the soil. Water from the bottom by setting the pot in a pail of water halfway up to the rim and waiting until the water has reached the top of the soil. Lift it out right away and let it drain thoroughly. Cover the top with a plastic cover or else repeat the watering process again when you see the soil getting dry. The idea is to keep the seeds moist so they can germinate. Keep the pots in a semi-shady spot until you see little sprouts coming up. Then move them to the permanent sunny location. As with vegetables, thinning the seedlings has to be done in order to have strong, healthy plants, so leave only a few of these in the pot, spaced well apart. Obviously, choose to keep those seedlings which are the most advanced and vigorous in their growth. Unfortunately, this is what is meant by survival of the fittest in horticulture! The future belongs to the young and the strong.

Which herbs to raise depends on (1) which pre-started plants are available and (2) your personal choice. Some suggestions for indoor growing are: tarragon, mint, rosemary, dill, thyme, chives, parsley, basil, summer savory, sage, sweet marjoram. Since so much depends on individual indoor location and climate, I suggest experimenting. Try as many as you can—or as you wish—and be guided by the results you get. After this, stick with your successes and forget the failures. If you spot any bugs, and you will (white flies adore *my* herbs), take the pot to the kitchen sink, cover the soil with foil and dunk the whole plant in lukewarm water. If you suspect aphids or any other pests, add some soap to the water and swish the plant about. Let it stand for an hour or so, and then rinse under water.

Unlike vegetables, herbs are very decorative when fully grown and healthy, and if planted in goodlooking pots, they can be placed elsewhere besides the kitchen. Herbs set on trays filled with pebbles can be displayed on the window sill of the dining room, or on glass shelves in a window of a family room, or on a wicker table in an enclosed, heated sunporch. Rosemary is especially attractive, resembling a small bush in its mature state. Try your hand at topiary by growing a young rosemary plant to a single stem and then allowing it to become full at the top, trimming the ends off (and using them for cooking) in order to maintain a nice round "head."

There doesn't appear to be much of an in-between when it comes to herbs. For each person who claims that for him they grow like weeds, there's another who has been disappointed and couldn't even claim success with chives. If you happen to be among the lucky ones who can grow herbs beautifully and you have just the right exposure for them, you might consider capitalizing on this good fortune. Even if "the right spot" happens to be the living room, where one would not ordinarily think of putting herbs, have a goodlooking planter built to fit in the area the plants find so much to their liking—on the window sills or on the floor if it's a glass wall, or around a bay window. Have the planter lined with a waterproof galvanized metal container and fill it with soil. Plant herbs directly into the soil for best results and an interesting design. Some herbs grow upright and others hang, so that you will have an unusual landscape effect. When it comes to the mints, however, keep them in pots; otherwise they sprawl all over the place, taking over the other herbs' territory. Or else insert a piece of metal or fiberglass in the planter to act as a divider between the mints and the other herbs.

Outdoors, most herbs prefer full sun, but some like partial shade. However, everything is more intense outdoors, including sunshine, so indoors you needn't have worries about too much light. Place the herbs in the brightest window you have and chances are that the light will be adequate. Obviously, a dark window won't do, nor will the hottest window of a home in the Southwest. Artificial light is the only solution to the first, and some sort of window shading is needed to cope with the second.

The main reason for herbs usually being relegated to the kitchen is convenience: it's handy for the cook to snip a bit of this or that when preparing a dish. But there's really nothing to prevent you from putting a pot of herbs right in the middle of an indoor garden filled with house plants if the area is sunny enough. When chives bloom you've never seen prettier lavender-blue flowers!

BULBS

This is the only bit of "cheating" that will be done in this book, because bulbs do not really belong in the permanent indoor garden. Hardy bulbs can be forced to bloom indoors earlier than they would normally outdoors, but the flowers last a short time. For the average apartment dweller who probably does not have a room which is kept at 40 degrees during the winter months, or extra room in the refrigerator to give the bulbs their "cold period," all this does not seem to be worth the bother. For homeowners with an unheated garage or sunporch or outside facilities, it's easy to force bulbs.

There is nothing which lifts one's spirits more on a cold, cloudy winter day—after weeks of the same—than seeing a mass of colorful daffodils and tulips bringing the promise of spring, giving us a taste of what is to come in a few weeks. I urge city dwellers to buy a few pots; call it extravagance, but I call it therapy for the soul and the senses. Florists have a plentiful supply of forced bulbs in late winter, so treat your indoor garden to a breath of spring. If you have a grouping of foliage plants, buy several small pots of daffodils, hyacinths and tulips, and mix them with the others. Or put all the bulbs together on a table and frame them with pots of ivy.

You get a truly smashing effect if you group the bulbs in one area, rather than putting one pot here and another there. A vivid splash of color is what you want, and this can only be done by grouping everything together in one spot. Surrounding them with greenery gives the design a naturalistic effect and sets off the plants effectively. Always buy plants that are not yet in full bloom so you may get the longest pleasure from them. They do best in bright light, but not in direct sun. Of course, a great deal depends on which part of the country you live in. Winter sun in many areas is very weak and of short duration during the day, while it's strong in the southern and southwestern states.

Now for the house dwellers who want to force their own bulbs instead of buying them at the florist, here is the procedure:

First: in October, buy the best bulbs available at your garden supply center. These are often called "exhibition" varieties, and will be labeled as to which ones are for forcing. Smaller bulbs used for bedding purposes produce very small flowers when forced; others may not flower at all. Since you will be buying just a few, buy the best.

Bulbs which are good for forcing are crocus, hyacinth, daffodil (narcissus), tulip, snowdrop and grape hyacinth. Don't mix them in the same pot. For best effect, stick to a pot of yellow tulips, another pot of pink tulips, one of a special kind of daffodils, another of only white narcissus with reddish centers, and so forth.

Second: buy clay "bulb pans," aptly named! These are the wide-topped, squat pots made especially for potting bulbs, although they have other uses as well, so keep them after you discard the bulbs. They're great for begonias, which have shallow root systems.

The size of the pot depends on the impact you want to create, because the larger the pot the more bulbs you can plant, obviously. If they're to be displayed by themselves, say three or more pots together, get the larger sizes. If you're going to mix them with other plants, the smaller pots are better. Figure roughly that a four- or five-inch pot takes two or three daffodils or tulips, twice that number of the smaller bulbs (like grape hyacinth and crocus), and one hyacinth, which needs the most room because of the large size of its flower. A seven-inch pot holds three hyacinths, six daffodils or tulips, and about a dozen of the smaller bulbs.

Third: make a batch of potting soil mixture #1. It already has bone meal among its ingredients, which is excellent for the growth of bulbs.

Fourth: place a layer of drainage material at the bottom of the pot, and then the soil. Plant bulbs so that they are just barely touching. (You wouldn't do this outdoors, but the idea here is to get a lush, full look.) Plant the bulbs with their tops facing up. Unlike some plants (such as caladium tubers) which test one's sanity trying to figure out which is the bottom and which the top, these hardy bulbs make it easy for you. The top is pointed. The flat end is the bottom. (Many beginners are never told what appears to be so obvious to seasoned gardeners, and they merrily proceed to push all the pointed ends into the soil.) Leave part of the tops showing. Firm the soil around each bulb, and moisten the entire pot gently but thoroughly.

Position bulbs all around the rim of the pot as well as in the center—if it's a large pot. Also, the size of the bulbs determines how many can fit into the pot. The figures given earlier are only a rough indication. If you're left with one of everything, plant each in its own small pot. Bring in one pot at a time and set it on the kitchen table where it will bring smiles to the breakfast crowd.

Fifth: place the pots anywhere that will not become warmer than 45 to 50 degrees. Hardy bulbs need a period of six to eight weeks to break dormancy and start the growth of good roots. This is the reason for the cold period. There are several ways you can keep your bulbs cold: an unheated garage, an unheated sunporch, a dark basement, a stone well around a tree (cover the pots with a thick layer of *loose* leaves or hay—don't pack it down), a trench (also covered with a thick layer of leaves or sand), or a cold frame if you have one.

Whichever method you choose to keep the bulbs cold, *but not frozen,* remember that they have to be kept moist and that therefore you must have access to water. Going out in winter weather with a watering can is not going to predispose you to forcing bulbs the following year. Try to find a convenient spot where you can keep an eye on their growth and attend to their watering needs. I keep mine lined up on either side of our unheated garage with a layer of very fine wire mesh on top to keep the mice from having delicious meals. Fortunately, the hose, which is kept connected all winter, reaches from the nearby greenhouse to the garage so that I can water the pots easily, every two weeks or so.

Sixth: Starting with the first week in January or thereabouts, depending on the date you potted the bulbs, start bringing the pots indoors. Some will have quite a bit more growth showing than others, so bring these in first. But how you do it is really up to you. Some prefer to bring in one or two pots at a time, spacing them two weeks apart so that they have bulbs in bloom over a long period. Others prefer the go-all-the-way approach, wanting one tremendous show of spring flowers, especially if a special occasion such as a birthday or dinner party is coming up.

When you first bring the pots indoors, do not place them in warm areas if at all possible. A semi-shady, cool spot is what they need—around 60 degrees is ideal. As the shoots start to grow higher and turn green, move the pots gradually to a lighter location, until finally you have them in your brightest spot.

Seventh: forced bulbs cannot be forced another year but, contrary to many opinions, they can be planted outdoors with good results. This is not to say that all will come up the following year, but if even only half live, it's far better than throwing them away. I have planted all of my prize "exhibition" bulbs on a wooded slope, and some have been spectacular. So plant them outside or give them to friends, who will be most appreciative.

Plants in the Office

Large corporations, banks, hotels, shopping centers and department stores are all aware of the value of plants. In recent years, plant sales to commerce and industry have skyrocketed.

Plants are used not only to decorate an area, but also to define traffic patterns, reduce the noise level, replace standard partitions in large offices and convey a cooling tranquil feeling in a busy world. Architectural eyesores are cleverly camouflaged by plants, both indoors and outdoors. And most important, plants bring warmth to what is usually an impersonal atmosphere—a structure of glass and steel erected for the no-nonsense purpose of conducting business. The friendly public "image" that has become a primary concern with industry has a friend and ally in the world of plants. A potential customer is favorably influenced—even if subconsciously—by friendly and attractive surroundings that are not overpowering or chillingly antiseptic, and what better way to achieve this than with plants? Employees respond favorably to surroundings which bring a touch of the outdoors to often windowless working areas. Green has proven in tests to be a soothing, restful color. This factor may not directly affect productivity, but it certainly is important in keeping morale and spirits high.

The designers of lobbies, reception rooms, executive suites in skyscraper office buildings, gigantic shopping malls, all have the money and the good sense to hire experts in the field of landscaping to plan and maintain elaborate indoor gardens. Landscape architects, or landscape designers, work closely with interior designers and architects to achieve harmonious results. If artificial lighting is needed, the landscape expert is on hand to advise the architect where it should be installed—and he also influences the designs of the interior decorator as to which plants are suitable for each area and what are the proper containers for them.

My purpose in this chapter is not to discuss these types of indoor gardens, since they would not be executed by beginners or amateurs in the horticultural field. I know that sometimes the results make one wonder if the mother-in-law of the chairman of the board didn't get it all together, but this could

To keep the spacious look, yet with a hint of privacy, this office has used rows of low files and live greenery. The high level of fluorescent light available to the plants should keep them green and healthy. (*General Electric Company photograph*)

be from lack of proper communication and coordination among the various experts hired.

Rather, I have in mind the small businessmen and women, professionals, shopkeepers, restaurateurs, who want something "green" in their place of work. More often than not, it's the wife or the secretary who's asked to go out and buy a few plants to perk up the place a bit. I have included photographs of large, professionally-designed indoor gardens to illustrate the many possibilities of decorating with plants in commercial surroundings, and to give the reader a chance to see how the experts do it, perhaps pick up one or two of their tricks, and study the grouping of plants. Scale is important as it relates to the plant and the size of its container—and to the size of the area; for this, illustrations tell the story far more effectively than words.

What are some of the guidelines in using plants in a business environment?

Climate control. There is none of it for plants. The temperature is set for the comfort of people in the building—sometimes the individual in his own private office can't open his window (if he has one) and there is no individual thermostat to raise or lower the temperature. Mostly, this is a big plus for plants, because offices tend to be somewhat cooler than apartments. Of course, the way the energy crisis has forced temperatures down is the best thing that ever happened to plants—and people as well.

However, at night, and on weekends and holidays, the temperature is lowered to somewhere between 50 and 60. Many plants of tropical origin will not tolerate this much cold. Drafts are frequent, as people keep opening and closing doors to offices. Climate conditions should be looked upon as something that can't be changed, and to which the plants must simply adapt themselves. Much emphasis must be placed, therefore, on the proper location and selection of plants.

Location of plants. The same common sense that prevails in the placement of plants in the home applies to the office. Keep plants away from radiators, air-conditioning outlets, hot air grills and fans. Cold air from an air conditioner constantly blowing on a plant will kill it in no time. So will the heat in front of a glass wall facing south, with no transparent window shade or drapery to partially screen out the rays of the summer sun. Unless there is artificial lighting, a dark corner is not desirable either; there must be *some* light.

Containers for plants. This is the most neglected item! I have been in offices of interior decorators and have seen plants in the most unsightly containers. Whatever clay pot the plant was in when purchased is the same one it's in now, with roots growing out the bottom hole or twisted on the surface. On the desk in another office, I saw a plant set on an ashtray "saucer," but at a somewhat precarious angle because the ashtray was too small for the pot. And this was the reception room of a prestigious firm!

Select a goodlooking, watertight container a few inches wider and deeper than the pot the plant is in now, and double-pot. Put moss in the space between the two pots to keep the plant's roots cool and create additional humidity. Add more moss on the surface.

For large containers, a mulch such as gravel, or redwood or pine bark nuggets, may be used instead of the moss. A mulch is not only beneficial to the plant, but adds tremendously to its looks. Always set the inner pot on a layer of pebbles to absorb drainage excess.

If you do not double-pot the plant, get a matching saucer to catch the drainage water. Buy a large saucer and fill it halfway with pebbles, so you can set the pot on top of it. As the water collects in the saucer, it keeps the pebbles moist, which in turn creates needed additional humidity.

Drainage is vitally important, and this is where you are at the mercy of the plant shop. Every plant should have a layer of drainage material inside the bottom of the pot—the bigger the pot, the deeper the layer. Many plant shops skip or forget this procedure, or frugally place only one small piece of clay over the drainage hole. Considering the cost of large plants today, you are entitled to a properly potted plant. Take a long stick with you to the shop, and insert it clear down to the bottom of the plant, along the side of the pot so as not to disturb the roots. If you feel nothing, if it's nice and smooth as you move the stick a bit, I would question the owner of the shop regarding the drainage layer. What you should feel is a gritty, bumpy response to the probing of the stick.

With small plants, you're better off repotting them yourself. If you've bought the plant in a fancy store and the pot is new and clean, simply knock the plant out of the pot (by gently tapping the sides of the pot against any surface) and see if there are bits of clay or gravel at the bottom. If so, just put the plant back, firm the soil, and water. If drainage is lacking, add a layer of broken bits of clay, gravel or pebbles bought at pet shops, and replant. If the plant's roots are filling up most of the pot, you might as well repot it to one size larger now and save yourself work later on.

Some cut-rate plant shops have good foliage plants suitable for offices, but these come in old, dirty clay pots that require a great deal of hard work to get clean again. Chances are that the plant will be pot-bound as well, so buy a new container a size larger and repot the plant properly. Don't forget the matching saucer.

Selection of plants. Let's be realistic. Plants in office or commercial establishments will not receive tender, loving care. People are too busy to be gardeners during their working day. Therefore, only plants that are virtually foolproof should be selected. This means foliage plants—as opposed to flowering ones—and those needing low to medium light.

Many of the plants listed on the Specimen and Foliage Charts (see pages 170-189) are suitable. These include palms, ferns, dracaenas, bromeliads, Chinese evergreens, self-heading philodendrons, grape ivy and spathiphyllum. Not to be overlooked for sunny areas are large specimens of cacti and succulents. They are used to the hot days and cool nights of the desert, and can go for longer periods without watering. But for the sake of creating a handsome decorative accent, get the mature, large plants. They will last for many years and the maintenance is just about zero (who dusts a cactus?).

When selecting a plant, keep it in scale with the office or the area where it will be placed. There's a touch of science-fiction in the sight of a man behind a desk in a small room with an enormous plant that seems to be growing larger by the day and threatening a takeover. The average office can take one good-sized plant in an important-looking container (see the chapter on con-

Using plants to define traffic patterns and to replace standard solid partitions is becoming increasingly popular in large companies, but seldom is it so dramatically utilized as in the offices of this firm. Walls of greenery curve their way in and out, creating pockets of privacy where needed. This concept is functional and beautiful and, from the psychological point of view, it fulfills the common need that office workers share for soothing, restful surroundings that have a touch of the outdoors. (*Photographs courtesy of The Carborundum Company, Niagara Falls, N.Y.*)

Most small private offices have room for one floor plant, if there is sufficient natural or artificial light. The graceful tree above is light and airy enough not to overpower the room, and is handsomely silhouetted against the vertical blinds. (*Photograph courtesy of Window Shade Manufacturers Association*)

ABOVE: These stately, formal trees add just the right touch to the sleek, elegant look of this reception room. (*Photograph courtesy of Hugh M. Keiser Associates, Inc.*)

BELOW: The complaint most often heard about ultramodern, super-functional offices is that they are cold-looking. The simplest way of "humanizing" working areas is to bring in large tubs of lush, green foliage plants. The magic of nature works instantly. (*Photograph courtesy of The Space Design Group*)

tainers for excellent examples), and/or a row of several plants on a table which holds magazines or company literature.

Where plants are grouped together, have them in similar containers, such as four five-inch ceramic pots with matching saucers, or watertight containers which hold pot and plant inside. The latter prevents worries about water spilling over the saucer, or dust and dirt collecting in it, not to mention visitors who use plant saucers as ashtrays! However, check periodically to see that excess water does not remain at the bottom of the container.

Maintenance. If the time is taken initially to pot a plant properly—in the correct container—with a mulch on the surface and more down the sides between the clay pot and the outside container, maintenance should be minimal. The mulch conserves moisture inside the plant, thereby allowing less frequent watering. By putting a layer of pebbles at the bottom of the outside container and setting the plant on top of it, as already mentioned,

Solid partitions could have been used to form the sides of this conference area, but how much more cheerful and airy it is with plants instead! The feeling of privacy is still preserved. (*Photograph courtesy of The Space Design Group*)

An alternative to murals is a grouping of plants for a large blank wall. This is an excellent example of the proper use of plants in such a location: architecturally exciting foliage, varying heights, matching styles of containers, and asymmetrical placement. (*Photograph courtesy of The Space Design Group*)

Banks are pioneers in the artistic use of plants. An elevator lobby is matched in its boldness of design by striking exotic plants. This is a clever way to decorate empty space. (*Photograph courtesy of The Space Design Group*)

Showrooms have to have glamour, *pizzaz*! Plants highlight rather than compete with a striking decor. To make a "statement," enough plants of important proportions should be grouped together. This principle applies to any large indoor garden. (*Photograph courtesy of The Space Design Group*)

you will almost eliminate danger from water sitting there too long. This is an additional precaution worth taking with double-potting anywhere—in the home or in the office. Roots quickly rot if they're left standing in water, so you have the choice of checking after each watering or putting in a layer of pebbles. I prefer the latter method.

Because most plants in commercial settings tend to be much larger than those usually found in homes, less frequent watering is needed. Large containers, holding much more soil, dry out more slowly than do small ones. The finger test is again good here. If the soil feels damp to the touch, two or more inches below the surface, don't water. If it's powdery dry, water thoroughly and don't repeat until it's dry again. After you've done this a couple of times, you'll know the pattern of your plants, and you won't have to go around poking your finger inside pots all the time. If in doubt, it's always better not to water, and wait a few more days. Don't think that because cacti are desert plants they don't ever need watering. They need far less than others, but do need some water about every two to three weeks—but again, check the soil moisture first.

Much is made of "room temperature" water for plants. But where does one get any in the average office? The water cooler is usually the nearest source of water. If the ladies' or men's rooms are close by, this is obviously where you'll fill the watering can. However, if the water cooler is temptingly near, don't be fearful about using it. My husband's office has many plants, and they have always been watered with ice-cold water from his cooler. A short trip down the hall could easily bring them warmer water from the men's room, but laziness wins out, and the cooler is the elected source. When I see the healthy results, I'm in no position to make snide remarks.

Also, my husband dislikes hot weather so much that his air conditioner is on from April through October (and this is in New York City, no less), keeping the temperature in the 65- to 68-degree range. His secretary doesn't much like it, but the plants certainly do! He relishes telling people that the secret to raising healthy plants is lots of ice-cold water and blasts of air conditioning. What can I say? Obviously plants adapt to certain situations, so don't be timid about trying unorthodox methods if these are the only ones at your disposal and if you keep on growing healthy plants.

Grooming plants involves removing dead leaves and any dead branches, and periodically dusting the leaves.

Last, but not least, some plants will die eventually. Be prepared to replace them as soon as this happens, as nothing is more unsightly than a dead plant in the middle of healthy ones. Even in the privacy of your own home this is not attractive, but at least only you and your family see it until the damage is repaired; in a business office (or doctor's reception room, or restaurant) visitors and clients notice it, and it certainly does not add to the firm's "image."

Fortunately, plants grown under low-light conditions need little fertilizing, so I haven't touched on this subject, knowing full well that the average businessman is not about to follow any fertilizing program. This is true of pruning as well. Pinching back certain plants is beneficial, but it won't get done in an office. Of course, if an office is lucky enough to have among its employees someone who grows plants at home and is knowledgeable about their culture, hang on to that person! But such a jewel is rare, so when plants get sickly-looking (not dead, mind you), give them to somebody who'll revive them and appreciate the gift, or take them home and have your spouse do it—and then go out and buy replacements.

All the gardens pictured here and on the following pages are *indoors*, under glass. These are not typical "offices," obviously, but they demonstrate the vast possibilities of indoor gardens. Designs of such grandiose scale nevertheless share similar principles with plantings in the home: adequate light and ventilation, careful mixture of interesting plant material, trailing plants to soften harsh lines, water to raise the humidity, and a knowing eye for the correct proportion of plants to their surroundings. (*All photographs courtesy of Everett Conklin Company, Inc. except for picture on page 141, courtesy of H. M. Keiser Associates, Inc.*)

CONTAINERS AND PLANT STANDS

WHETHER YOU'RE DEALING with container gardening outdoors or house plants indoors, the principle is the same: a plant grows in a pot instead of in the ground. As a result, containers have to be both functional *and* attractive, especially indoors, where they are decorative assets to their surroundings as well as to the plants. The wrong container ruins the looks of the handsomest plant, just as it makes a rather ordinary-looking plant seem special. In selecting a container, keep three factors in mind: the size of the plant, the interior design of the room where it is to be placed, and the function of the plant in the room. Let's take each point separately.

The size and shape of the container should be in pleasing proportion to the height and width of the plant. A tall plant in a tiny container, even if it has a small root ball (more later about how to get around that), is going to look out of balance. It's difficult to give a formula, such as that a container should be one-third of the height of the plant, because growth habit is a vital factor. Some plants are tall but skinny, others are tall and bushy, some are short and bushy, and so forth. Foliage is also a factor, delicate or bold. Flowing plants are usually more airy-looking than foliage ones. So, when it comes to proportion, nothing beats your own eye.

The size of the plant above the soil surface is not the only factor in determining the size of the container; what's below also counts. The roots are most important. They need plenty of room in which to breathe and grow without being squeezed, but they don't like to swim around either. You can tell at a glance if your plant is a slow grower or not. If, as with begonias, you have a fairly mature plant with plenty of foliage and flowers but a tiny root ball, you know it's a slow grower. A pot only large enough to hold the roots and soil comfortably is all that is needed. On the other hand, if you have a young spider plant, you'll quickly note that the roots are as bulky as the top of the plant. This one is a quick grower, make no mistake about that!

Now for the trick to fool the eye. In the ground outdoors (as all plants were meant to grow, after all) no one knows the size of the roots below the plant, so that balance in design is never a factor. But once the plant is in a pot, that's a different story. Not only will a bushy plant look top-heavy and funny in a tiny pot, even though the latter will hold its small roots adequately, but the plant will topple over at the slightest movement. Yet, it would be harmful to pot it in a much larger container. So simply double-pot it. Slip the pot and plant into a handsome larger container, one that's in correct proportion to the plant. Put a bed of gravel at the bottom of the outer container for drainage. Fill in the sides and surface with more gravel, marble chips or green moss. The inner container will disappear and the plant will seem to be growing out of the larger container. You'll be happy and the plant will be happy—and healthy as well.

The interior design of the room where the plant is to be located influences the style of the container. Is the room furnished principally in Early American, Contemporary, Traditional, Spanish, French, Victorian? Look for a container that reflects or complements the mood of the period. If one is difficult to find, or if you are in doubt about styles, choose a container with simple, classic lines or the forever-popular-with-good-reason red clay pot. Baskets are great anywhere. They can be quite expensive in the larger sizes necessary for tall plants, or if they are antiques, but they add warmth to any room decor. However, check that they are sturdy and well made. As shown in the illustrations on pages 144-146 and 152-153, there are still many more kinds of pots from which you can choose. Hunting down the right one is a fun job. Sometimes contrast can be dramatic, such as when a large ornate Victorian birdcage is used as a planter in a strictly contemporary room.

If a room is not furnished all in one style but is eclectic in mood, you have wonderful freedom in selecting the right container. The period of the furnishings does not hold you down as might, for instance, a roomful of antique eighteenth-century French furniture whose scale and proportions demand precise harmony. The guide for selecting a container for a room that has a "bit of everything" is suitability of pot to plant and, as we'll see, the function of the plant in the room.

Where a plant is to be placed and what it's supposed to contribute to the room are the last but important factors in selecting a container. Will the plant be displayed by itself as a dramatic accent? Will it be one of a number of plants in a corner or alongside a glass wall? Will it be part of a plant collection on glass shelves in a window or on an etagere? The plant is the star, the container only the supporting player. This is especially true when a

Courtesy of Architectural Pottery

Courtesy of Habitat

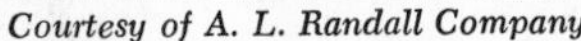

Courtesy of A. L. Randall Company

Courtesy of California Redwood Association

Containers are available today in all kinds of shapes, sizes, colors, and styles. Those without holes are for double-potting; others can be planted into directly. Select sleek, simple lines for containers to be used in contemporary rooms. Wood tubs are good planters anywhere for shrubs and trees.

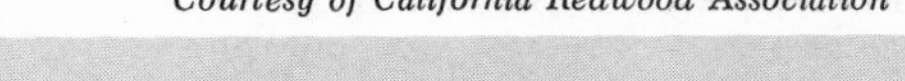

Courtesy of California Redwood Association

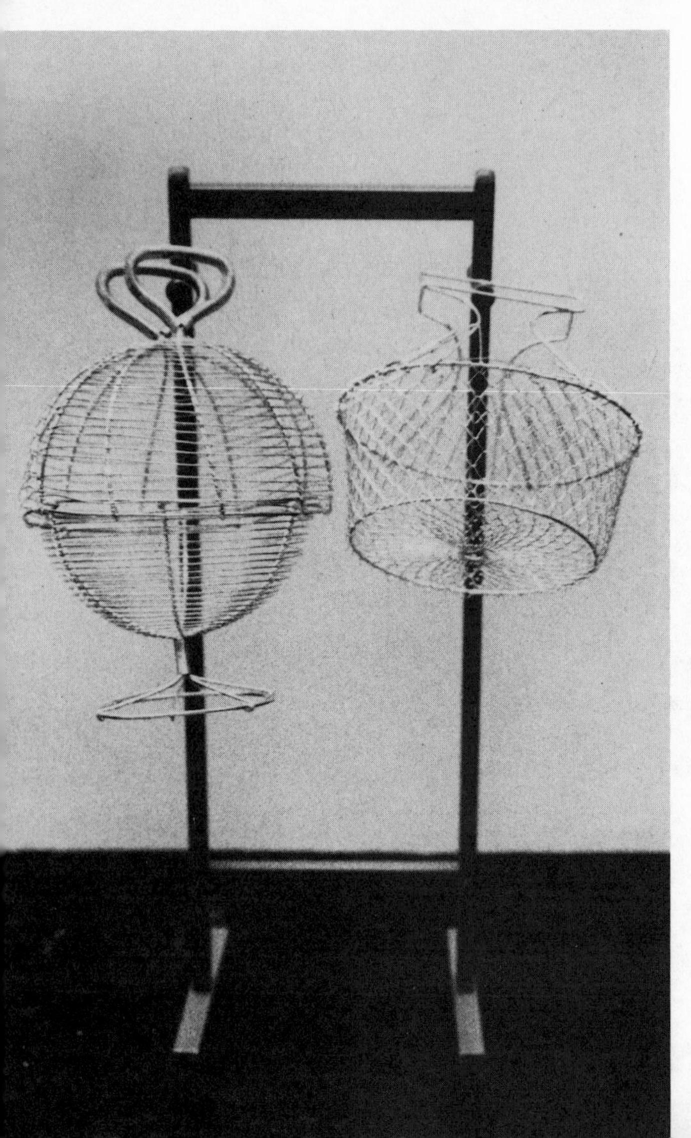

Let imagination run wild the next time you're going through a good Housewares department. Salad baskets are amusing for hanging plants in a kitchen. Bowls of all types are great for double-potting, using moss or fine mulch to hide the inner pot. Roasting pans double as trays to hold a collection of small pots. A metal rack normally used to hold pots and pans is an inventive way of displaying small hanging baskets of herbs. And there's more, lots more! (*Photographs by Brian Manning; houseware items courtesy of Bloomingdales, New York City*)

collection of plants is grouped together. The eye would reject the clutter of a dozen pots in different colors and designs on glass shelves, and not even notice the plants in them. In a shelf collection stick with the simplest pots and matching saucers. Sizes can be varied to suit the plants, but don't mix styles. Double-potting is prudent if there is danger of water overflowing the saucers onto a priceless rug or antique furniture. Not all saucers are completely waterproof. Unglazed clay collects moisture underneath and could stain a table top. In most cases, carefully lining the saucer with heavyweight aluminum foil or double-strength plastic does the trick.

Where three or four important plants are grouped together, more than one style of container can be introduced, so long as they harmonize. A tree needs a large container, such as a wood box or highfired clay planter, while a companion foliage plant, such as a schefflera, can be potted in a smaller container of the same style. The other plants grouped around these two can be in their own matching pots. As with mixing different patterns in a room, it takes a trained eye to pull it off. When combining several containers, it's best to stick with two styles at the most. There is no need to fear monotony from the use of similar pots, for plants are highly individualistic. Like people, they're different even when they have the same parents. A grouping of plants in clay pots wouldn't be boring. Look around a nursery or a flower shop if you're in doubt. Note the immense variety in the shape and texture of the leaves, the flowers, the colors, the branching habits—there's no end.

What about the specimen plant, carefully selected as the one dramatic accent in a room? Obviously, nothing but the handsomest container will do here. Since both plant and container are on display, take your time in choosing both, for they'll represent a sizeable investment. If it's a flowering plant, a solid color container is best, rather than a flowery pattern or anything overly ornate. Fancy containers are best limited to foliage plants. But whether solid or patterned, a container for a specimen plant should adhere to the same basic guidelines already discussed: a container should be in proportion to the plant and in harmony with the style of room furnishings.

A word about the "personality" of the plant in relation to its container. We've discussed the style of the room, the proportions of container to plant, the function of the plant in the room. But what about the personality of the plant? It, too, has to be taken into consideration. Take a giant cactus. *There's* a bold, dramatic accent! It certainly wouldn't look at home in a fragile, French porcelain jardiniere. Baskets or clay planters set off this family of plants best. On the other hand, the formal-looking standard or espalier is a striking sight in that type of jardiniere.

Plants have very definite personalities and this intangible factor should be considered in choosing a container. It makes the difference between a merely suitable container for a particular plant, and a smashing one. Fortunately, containers can be found in varieties to match many moods: bold, delicate, romantic, elegant, formal, casual, and so forth.

My personal opinion about "cutie" containers is that they are best left alone. Ivy growing out of a coffee grinder or a geranium sprouting from the skull of a figurine does neither the plant nor the container any justice. Each vies for attention and good taste is the loser. Good taste is highly subjective, yet it's the thin line that separates imaginative use of containers and contrived "cuties." In a kitchen the use of cooking utensils to hold plants is amusing because it's witty and appropriate. (See illustrations on page 146.) In a living room, these same planters would be out of place. By all means let your imagination run wild, that's the fun part of choosing containers—but keep in the back of your mind the setting in which plant and container will find themselves. Artsy-crafty pots smack of souvenir shops. Leave these to nostalgia collectors.

Pots and Tubs. The selection of containers in local stores depends a good deal on the area in which you live. Some can only be purchased through interior designers, landscape designers or architects. Most can be obtained locally or through mail order.

By far the most popular pot for small to medium-sized plants is the brick-red clay pot. As mentioned, its color mellows with age and fits into almost any room. It's also the healthiest pot for most plants because clay, being porous, allows the roots to breathe and absorb water readily. It releases moisture, saving the plant from overwatering. Any unglazed clay pot should be soaked in water overnight before being used, to prevent the pot from absorbing moisture from the plant.

If you have a large number of plants grouped together, you can't beat the common clay pot. It comes in three shapes: "standard," "azalea" and "bulb pan." Standard is as wide on top as it is high; thus, a two-inch pot measures two inches across the top and it's two inches high. (All pot sizes are measured across the inside top.) Azalea pots are three-quarters as high as they are wide. For most plants, this shape is preferable. Check to see which of your plants are slow-growing and do not have a large root system. This type of pot will be better suited for them. The bulb pan is obviously best suited for bulbs, but also may be used for any shallow-rooted plant. They're about half as high as they are wide. All of these pots come with matching saucers, but both pot and saucer are porous, so be careful where you place them. Seldom is every size available in each of the three shapes, but the range is usually from the tiny seedling size, one and one-fourth inch, to the twenty-four-inch tub size. Clay is heavy, especially after the plant has been watered, so it's best to consider where the plant will be placed before you decide on a clay pot.

There is a streamlined version of the popular clay pot. Sometimes called

Italian or villa, it comes in "high" and "low" styles. The rim at the top is almost nonexistent. For those wanting clay with a more contemporary look, this is an excellent pot. It comes in sizes from three to twenty inches, with matching saucers. Incidentally, clay pots are cheaper by the dozen in most places when you're purchasing many of the same size.

There are several other styles of unglazed clay pots. The well-known strawberry jar is one. It's attractive planted with herbs, succulents or cacti, or just about anything that hangs and makes an interesting pattern against the red clay background. Watering is tricky with the larger jars. For this reason, inserting a length of perforated plastic hose down the center of the potting soil is a wise idea. The water seeps through evenly, all the way down. There are squat strawberry jars and tall ones. There are also barrel-shaped pots, three-legged pots, pots shaped like animals (go easy on these, they can get to be "cuties"), and others.

Some clay pots may be bought already painted white or green, but you can do this easily with enamel house paint. While still new, clean and dry, clay pots can be "dressed up" with any Contac design cut to fit the pot, or with bamboo or green cloth. Obviously, the porous quality of the clay will be diminished or totally eliminated with the application of any of these materials.

Now for the disadvantages of the clay pot. It breaks easily; when it does, save the bits and pieces to use as drainage material. It's hard to clean. A green mold forms on the outside when the plant is overfertilized or in a damp place. This must be scrubbed off with warm water and soap. (There are products made to remove green mold for up to six months without harm to the plant.) Plants dry out quickly in a clay pot, so that they should be looked at frequently and given the "finger" test to check whether watering is indicated. (This means sticking your finger into the soil: if dry, water; if damp to the touch, leave alone.) And lastly, a clay pot is heavy, making it an unwise choice where several are to be grouped on a fragile stand or hung from a precarious ceiling.

The plastic pot has none of these disadvantages. It's light and practically unbreakable (that is, if you don't drop it or pick it up by the rim with one hand when it's filled with soil). It's non-porous, so the plant doesn't need watering as often. It comes in white or colors, although I think bright colors clash with plants. The transparent plastic pot, however, is smart-looking and blends into the background. Whether it's in clear or smoke-colored transparent plastic, the dark soil turns the pot into an invisible mass. This is a great pot to use inside decorative rope hangers, because the cascading plant is the only thing one sees from a few feet away. A word of caution on these: some plants may resent having their roots exposed to light. Repot in an opaque pot if the plant appears sickly.

Plastic pots also come with their own saucers, which are waterproof. A large pot can tip over if the plant is very tall; if the plant is short but bushy, danger is not so great. The best bet with any large plastic pot is to put it inside a heavy decorative planter. (This is true also of styrofoam pots, which are waterproof but air porous and very lightweight, resembling clay pots in appearance.) Another advantage of plastic pots is that they are easily washed in soapy water with household bleach added to sterilize the pot against pests and diseases.

The disadvantage of non-porous plastic pots is that if one has the tendency to overwater plants, their roots will rot quickly since there is no way for excess moisture to escape except through the drainage holes. However, this factor turns into a plus for people who travel a good deal or who water their plants spasmodically. It's also a boon to those with weekend homes, who can only check on their plants once a week. You can even make it through two weeks if you set the plastic pots on saucers filled with pebbles and water. But worry-birds who keep watering their plants every day should stay away from plastic pots in general. Clay pots will give their plants a fighting chance to escape drowning.

I find that while I prefer plastic pots for cutting down my watering chores, I much prefer the looks of clay. So indoors and on the terrace, I double-pot the plastic inside the clay. Purely for the sake of looks (since plastic is non-porous), I fill in the space between the two pots with sphagnum moss, finishing the top with green moss. (Green sheet moss is quite expensive, so I save it for where it shows, using the other moss as a base.) When double-potting a *clay* pot inside a jardiniere, keep the moss moist so the plant can absorb the needed moisture directly through the porous clay walls.

There are many types of containers for specimen plants. Contemporary styles are striking, their classic lines perfect for certain plants. Some of these modern planters are made of high-fired clay in unglazed white or glazed in colors; of fiberglass (which is virtually impervious to scratching, chipping, or discoloration) in white or colors; or of Synceram, a new material which is strong and durable and also comes in many colors. Containers made of concrete and similar mixtures are too heavy for indoor use, except those in very small sizes. Weight becomes a problem when larger-sized pots are required. For this reason, wood is generally preferred when trees are involved.

There are planters with built-in casters and an excess "water reservoir," which acts as a saucer to catch drainage water. Some planters come with or without drainage holes, so specify which you want. There are even models with carpet vents, which allow air to circulate under the container to prevent carpet damage! Weight is always a factor to consider when selecting containers for an apartment or a house. When filled with plant and soil, and watered, even a medium-sized pot becomes surprisingly heavy.

One can also choose soy tubs (made of wood and bamboo), glazed pots and planters made from decorative tiles. The many patterns available in imported tiles make for striking designs. Shallow, three-legged clay pots are perfect for succulents and cacti. So are pans made of brown pottery. The list is virtually endless. As previously mentioned, not everything is available everywhere, and much depends on locality and demand. The latter is going up at a formidable rate due to the galloping interest in indoor gardens.

In addition to the larger contemporary containers already described, consider wood tubs for important shrubs and trees. Wood need not be rustic-looking, unless you choose it because of the country style of your furnishings. The popular hexagonal tubs, kegs and barrels are unsurpassed for outdoor use, but they look out of place in most living rooms. More suitable is the square or rectangular wood box with a "cap" or rim, which can be homemade or made-to-order by a carpenter. However, many garden supply centers carry wood tubs.

Cedar is a good wood to use, but redwood is longer-lasting. Both weather beautifully with age and also take to painting (wild colors are *not* recommended). Although these wood tubs resist rot, it's a good idea to line them with heavy black plastic, being careful to punch drainage holes at the bottom. This makes the tub non-porous, so keep this in mind when watering the plant. Dollies of matching wood are available and necessary with heavy plants. Green round wood tubs are also attractive and readily available in most localities.

Keep your eyes open next time you walk through the woods or along a beach if you want to collect some really one-of-a-kind containers! Cleaned tree stumps and driftwood make great planters for ferns, palms, bromeliads or orchids (for those who can't bear to be without these in the house). Soak them thoroughly to remove all traces of sea salt. Hollow out pockets in the wood and line them with waterproof trays, having them made to order if necessary. Hide the trays with moss after you've slipped the plants into their pots. There's something marvelously rewarding in finding or making your own container. The creative juices flow and you just *know* that no one else in the world has the very same thing. In this machine age, it's a good feeling.

Cache-Pots and Jardinieres. These are fancy French names for any plant container without drainage holes. For this reason, it's best never to plant directly in them, for it's playing horticultural Russian roulette to figure out how much water to give the plants, especially when it comes to very large containers. But they're fabulous as outer planters.

Keep the plant in its plastic or clay pot and simply slip it inside any jardiniere whose size and design are compatible with the plant and the decor of your home. Line the bottom of the jardiniere with a layer of pebbles mixed with some charcoal bits. This prevents the plant from having its roots

Courtesy of L. Paul Brayton, Ltd.

Courtesy of Architectural Pottery

Courtesy of A. L. Randall Company

Courtesy of Elon, Inc.

Courtesy of Architectural Pottery

Call them containers, pots, planters, jardinieres or cache-pots, there is one to suit the mood of every home, no matter what the style. Those made of decorative tiles are especially effective with desert plants in Mediterranean-type interiors.

Courtesy of A. L. Randall Company

Courtesy of A.L. Randall Company

Courtesy of Gottscho-Schleisner

Courtesy of Architectural Pottery

sit in water, should you overdo it. The charcoal keeps everything smelling sweet. Fill in the space between the two pots with a mulch of sphagnum moss, topping off the surface with ornamental pebbles, marble chips, finely shredded bark or green moss. Mulching in this manner conserves moisture, keeps the plant cooler in summer and is goodlooking besides.

Jardinieres and cache-pots (the latter are smaller-sized jardinieres meaning literally "hide-pot") can be found in antique shops, garden supply centers, mail order houses, department stores and your great-aunt's attic. Some examples of items which can serve as jardinieres: Japanese porcelain urns, old copper kettles, new or antique baskets with waterproof liners (for large plants, check to see that the basket is sturdy enough—otherwise it will get lop-sided quickly), cast iron pots, ceramic tubs (without holes), tole baskets, birdcages (sink pots into a waterproof base covered with green moss or pebbles). Care must be taken with any metal container because it can get extremely warm under strong sunlight. Save aluminum, brass or copper containers to use in the shadier spots of the home. Obviously, there are jardinieres and cache-pots manufactured specifically for the purpose of holding plants, but why limit yourself only to these? It's more fun to create your own!

Do not buy a jardiniere that fits your potted plant like a glove. There should be *at least* half an inch between the two pots for air circulation to reach down to the bottom layer of pebbles. If more than one pot is put inside a jardiniere (such as two or three ferns inside a large copper urn), a mulch becomes imperative so as to have the whole design unified and attractive. A small "garden" can be created inside any extra-wide container. If one of the plants looks sickly, it's easy to pull out the pot and replace it with another while the "patient" is taken behind the scenes to recover. Proportion of plants to container is of special importance. A lot of small plants in a huge container look out of balance. Have at least one tall one and others of varying heights.

If you have doubts that your jardiniere is waterproof, line the bottom with extra-thick plastic or heavy-duty aluminum foil before spreading the layer of pebbles. Tiny, invisible cracks in old porcelain or pottery can allow moisture to seep out and stain carpeting, so line the jardiniere to be on the safe side.

In no other phase of indoor gardening is it possible to utilize one's imagination as much as when selecting a container for a plant. After all, when it comes to choosing the plant itself, one is greatly limited by such factors as light, temperature, and others. But when choosing a jardiniere, only its harmony with the room's furnishings and its proportions to the size of plant have to be considered. Within these criteria there are dozens of styles from which we can select.

Plant Stands. The function of a plant stand is to group plants together off the floor, not only creating a charming indoor garden scene, but making it much easier for the gardener to take care of his plants. One well-known plant stand is the tall wood or wrought iron Victorian stand which can hold only one plant (usually a cascading Boston fern). Today's version of this stand is a tall column made of Plexiglas or some other plastic, or done in a bamboo style. Whether Victorian or modern, a single-plant stand dramatizes a prize specimen beautifully.

Among planters made to hold many plants, none have been as consistently popular as the two- or three-tier wrought iron stand. It's light and airy-looking and does not compete with plants for attention. It's available in ornate designs that are faithful copies of last century's models, or in simple, contemporary lines. Plain clay pots with matching saucers are best with these planters, but whatever the style of the pots, they should all match and be spotless. Wood stands are found in department stores and antique shops. Some have a bamboo look; others come in different wood finishes.

Shops which specialize in plastic furnishings have some very attractive pieces which can be put to use as plant stands. For example, there is a folding rack with butler-tray top that can hold about six small pots. With several large plants grouped around its base on the floor, it becomes a charming mini-garden. Another idea is the stepladder in clear Lucite; it's the modern version of the traditional library stepladder, which would also make a great plant stand. But whichever is used, two small pots can fit on each rung, on both sides, plus a few pots on the top step. This takes care of quite a few plants! Add a couple of tall ones on either side, and it also makes an attractive indoor garden. Again, all pots should have matching saucers. Also available is a contemporary plastic stand shaped somewhat like a coat rack, with "hands" extending to the sides. It's quite similar to the well-known African violet stand, but totally modern in mood. Plants are shown to excellent advantage in such a situation, and obviously only those at their peak of beauty should be displayed.

No matter what kind of stand is used, variety in plant design is important in order to break up any possible monotony of line. Try a few trailing plants mixed with upright ones, flowering teamed with foliage plants, and differences in height (this can be achieved by putting a plant on top of an upside-down pot).

Basins sold as indoor garden pools make excellent floor planters. They are waterproof, sturdy, well constructed of fiberglass or metal, and—when filled with a layer of attractive pebbles and pots of lush foliage plants—are a dramatic accent in any room. If the floor will support the weight, pools made of stone are handsomest. For the most naturalistic effect, place a basin against a wall of stone or brick, or against a trellis-patterned wallpaper. Have tall foliage plants as background. This makes for a stunning indoor garden. It's especially striking if you have a tile floor, or any flooring that has an outdoor look. Of course the pool can be used for its original purpose, in which case it becomes a water garden.

Lavabos, when part of an over-all design, can be the center of attraction. Fill them with pots of hanging foliage plants and "answer" them with groupings of plants on the floor beneath. This creates a vertical "vast pocket" garden.

Self-watering pots and larger planters fortunately exist for the forgetful and for the traveler. Some are quite goodlooking, and come in different sizes. But they are costly, only practical when few are needed; having to purchase a large number could run into an impressive sum of money. Their principle is based on a water reservoir at the bottom of the pot, which, through capillary action, is slowly fed to the roots of the plant as required. Some models can function on their own for up to three weeks, making it safe for popular gadabouts.

Photograph by Window Shade Manufacturers Association

Stands keep plants off the floor and group them attractively, as you can see on the following pages. Wrought iron and wicker are always popular and appropriate, but don't overlook glass, plastic or wood. Don't place a planter in front of a radiator except during the summer. Unless waterproof trays are built in, each pot must have a matching saucer to catch drainage water. (*Photographs courtesy of Window Shade Manufacturers Association, Dirk De Vries Enterprises, John Astin Perkins, A.I.A., A.I.D., Interiors, The Dramatic Life*)

Photograph by The Dramatic Life

Photograph by Dirk De Vries Enterprises

LIST OF PLANT MATERIAL

It's been said that any plant can be made to grow indoors if the gardener precisely duplicates the environment native to the plant. This is correct theoretically, but it's not practical. Only botanical gardens and certain commercial nurseries can approach success in duplicating tropical rain forests, arctic and desert climates, and others.

The gardening hobbyist will go to great lengths in order to cultivate the more temperamental house plants, but those people primarily interested in plants to decorate their homes do not wish to spend the time needed for this type of indoor gardening. For the dedicated gardener, there are books listing almost a thousand plants that may be grown indoors, but the home decorator can create handsome indoor gardens with a tiny fraction of that number.

There are "best sellers" in every field, and plants are no exception. The same plants will reappear again and again on all lists simply because they are popular, undemanding, attractive and easy to grow under difficult indoor locations. The plants I chose are not only easy to grow, but do not require the services of a Sherlock Holmes to purchase. Most are readily available in any good plant shop or nursery; others can be obtained through one of the better mail order firms.

I have divided plants into four categories: 1) for use as specimen plants (used alone for a dramatic accent), 2) foliage plants, 3) flowering plants and 4) plants for hanging baskets.

It cannot be stressed enough that while certain plants are difficult for the majority of indoor gardeners to grow, they may thrive for others. For this reason, an open mind should be kept—but at least the reader will have been warned. If a plant is not on any of my lists, that doesn't mean it's impossible to grow indoors, but rather that there are others easier to grow for the novice gardener. Baskets of tuberous begonias and of fuchsias are breathtaking sights, unbelievably beautiful at their peak of flowering. But they need certain culture requirements that most people are in no position to meet. Even when grown outdoors, these plants are fussy about temperature, light and humidity.

The same is true of orchids. For people who are willing to maintain the stringent fertilizing program necessary for their blooming, they will flower regularly. For most others, it's foliage only, and orchids are not noted for attractive foliage.

It is much more rewarding for the beginner who is interested mainly in a decorative effect to start with easy-to-grow plants, and to progress slowly to the more demanding varieties as his self-confidence and knowledge increase. Not that he may wish to progress. There is sometimes a supposition that simply because a plant is hardy, not fussy about culture requirements, it can't be as beautiful or as desirable as its temperamental sisters. This approach is unfortunate because it couldn't be more wrong. Frequently, those easy-to-care-for plants don't look their best because they're neglected orphans, since one knows they can take it.

Let's take some horticultural "orphans": the common philodendron, sansevieria, grape ivy, asparagus fern, wandering Jew, spider plant. These are all hard workers in the plant world, demanding comparatively little from their keepers. Yet, picture a full, well-tended basket of the ordinary, hanging philodendron, its leaves a healthy, shining green, cascading in a thick, full way, as it can if kept properly pinched back. It's as lovely a sight of greenery as nature has. Is there a more maligned plant than sansevieria? One of its common names is "mother-in-law tongue"! It's constantly seen in store windows, bone dry, horribly potted, coated with dust—yet still living and carrying on. Try babying it a bit and watch the results. Simply put several sansevierias by themselves in a handsome pot, and look, *really* look, at the shape, texture and color of the leaves. Are there any others quite like it? Isn't it nice to have this entirely different-looking plant as a foil for others? Its tall spike leaves are a pleasing contrast to the conventionally-shaped leaves of most other plants.

Grape ivy and asparagus fern would be collectors' items if they were really hard to grow. The richness of color and lushness of growth habit of the grape ivy make it a valuable hanging plant, and so does the soft, mist-like quality of the asparagus fern with its dainty foliage. Without them, we would be robbed of two of the most romantic-looking plants we can grow in our home.

Let's not take any plant for granted but cherish each one for its own merit, and if it should turn out to be amiable in its demands, let's love it all the more. For this reason, I've concentrated on those plants which are easy to grow and to buy. Why tempt you with a thousand plants, nine hundred of which are hard to find, let alone to cultivate?

Plants which I ruled out, no matter how handsome, are those requiring high humidity, to the degree that they must be sprayed once or twice a day. Our homes, even during the energy crisis with its lower indoor temperatures (which automatically increase the humidity), still do not meet these special requirements. Only if you are truly dedicated to a plant will you mist it daily, and then only if it happens to be located in an area where the spray won't stain the wall and furnishings.

I also ignored plants which are excessively susceptible to drafts and sudden changes in temperature, as when a door is opened for a few moments in winter. Obvious are those plants left out because they need extremely low or high temperatures, out of the range of the average home. It should be remembered that, unlike outdoors where people must adapt to the weather conditions, indoor climate is maintained for the comfort of the people living there twenty-four hours a day. In this case it is the plants which must conform to the conditions. Happily, there are many plants which do adjust to this environment, so indoor gardeners face no lack of supply.

HOW TO USE THE PLANT LISTING

I have tried to keep the lists of plants as easy to understand as possible, knowing how confusing elaborate charts can be, with subdivisions, footnotes, and so forth. I suggest that you follow this procedure: First, decide *where* you want your plants. Location determines amount of light plants will receive, as well as how much humidity and heat. Second, check off plants which will grow under these particular conditions. The type of soil and amount of watering they should get are within *your* control, so these factors need not enter into your selections at this point.

From those plants that are suitable for a specific location, choose one—or several—that can answer your decorating needs. Example: If both a bushy plant and a light, feathery one will be happy hanging in your bedroom window, pick the one that is bushy and full if you need to screen out an unpleasant view. If you want a cluster of plants on the floor to look pretty next to French doors, choose plants that go well with one another in foliage textures, colors, heights. Once you know which plants will fare well in a particular spot, it's only a matter of sticking with those which will do the job you want done.

Botanical names are listed as well as common names, so you can be sure of getting the exact plant you want when ordering. Many plant families have hundreds of varieties, some good for indoors and others not. Knowing which is which is vital, and only by using the proper botanical name can you avoid a mistake. You should be especially exact about names if you buy your plant from a mail order house.

When I mention "average" temperature, I refer to that found in most houses and apartments—around 70 degrees, 68 for those who are energy-crisis-conscious and can control their temperature, and 72 for those people accustomed to warmer rooms. Obviously, the cooler temperature is by far the better for plants as it also raises the humidity. "Above average" denotes 75 degrees or higher, while "below average" refers to less than 65, as might be found in enclosed porches or any area of a house which might have a large amount of glass. On sunless winter days, modern houses with entire walls of glass tend to be much cooler than other homes. Windy exposures are also noticeably cooler. On the other hand, areas near radiators and air ducts are warmer than elsewhere in the home. Borrow a few thermometers and check the temperature *at the same time* in various parts of your home where you intend to place plants. You might be surprised at what you'll find. Then select plants accordingly.

Unless you have a humidifier, not much can be done to alter the humidity in your home other than to place plants on trays or saucers filled with pebbles which are kept moist. Grouping plants together also increases humidity. As already mentioned, this is such a tricky element to control that I have refrained from listing plants which require a very high percentage of humidity in order to do well. According to hygrometers, 45 to 75 percent relative humidity is considered "normal"—anything below being "dry" and above, "humid," Most homes are closer to 30 percent and less in winter, so that I have gone by this more realistic scale. I call "average" humidity anything that's between 30 and 50. In certain parts of the country, the humidity is always higher than this, which is great for indoor plants. If I were to specify an ideal plant situation, I would call for a daytime temperature of 68 degrees, dropping to 55-60 at night, with a relative humidity of 40-60.

I have subdivided "Light Needs" into three categories: low, medium and bright. Each could be subdivided in turn, but this would only lead to unnecessary confusion. The difference between "bright-medium" and "low-bright" would be a bit like that between the well-known "half-empty" and "half-full." *Low light* means no sun coming through the window but enough light to cast some shadow. *Medium light* is a bright area with some direct sun for an hour or two a day. *Bright light* receives direct sun several hours a day—usually a south, southeast or southwest exposure.

There is no set rule by which one definitely can say which exposure can be expected to be good for certain plants. I had five windows that faced south in my city apartment and each one had a different "climate," in spite of being so close together. One window had glass curtains; in another room a window was half cut off by an air conditioner, making the area as shady as if it faced north; the next window had no screening; the fourth was also cut in half by an air conditioner, but being nearer the corner of the building it had more sunlight coming in; and the fifth window got the most sun and had no screening, except for a transparent shade which I pulled down on hot summer days. An entirely different set of plants grew in front of each of the five windows, so that it is foolish to have strict regulations based solely on exposure pertaining to what can grow. What matters is the actual amount of light and sun that comes through.

Also, light changes with the seasons. In the winter, when the rays of the sun are weakest, shade-loving plants can be placed in front of south windows without fear of disaster, but let a few months go by and it's quite another story. Plants will not live happily in any extreme of light conditions. A dark corner, as well as the burning rays of a hot summer sun intensified through window glass, will doom a plant. Use some kind of screen between the plants and the glass if you're going to keep plants in a window the year round. In the winter it's the cold and drafts that plants resent, and in the summer it's excessive heat that gets them.

All this is common sense, but we need to check up on ourselves once in a while. Plant fanciers do it automatically because for years they've been programmed to think of the plants' welfare on a continuing basis, but not so the novice indoor gardener who starts out primarily to decorate his home. It will come to him in time as he gets to know his plants—which ones succeed and why, or why not. The wise gardener is not stubborn. He sticks with what does well in his garden and does more of the same, without tilting with windmills and trying to grow what obviously won't thrive on his property. This is true indoors as well. Don't buy a dozen of the same plant until you've tried one and know that it's thriving. Try it in different spots of the house and if it just won't grow, forget it. The plant obviously has certain requirements that you can't meet in your particular "climate."

Use "Light Needs" as a gauge, but be flexible. You will note in books on house plants that by no means do all experts agree on what kind of lighting a particular plant may require. Two highly respected horticultural bulletins that I read disagree totally on where to put English ivy. One has it under "low" lights, the other under "bright"! So it goes with other plants. The truth is that many plants adapt quite nicely to different situations. I grow English ivy in my lowest-light window and also in my highest, and near one window that's in between. Wax begonias also do well under different light densities. By and large, ivy prefers the shade and begonias do too—but a couple of hours of sun a day won't upset them at all.

Plants which flower or have brightly colored leaves need much more direct sun than do foliage plants, so keep this in mind when selecting plants for a sunny window. Reserve flowering plants for this site, and grow foliage plants elsewhere. If you never get any direct sun, don't despair, because foliage plants are spectacular indoors and are more dramatic from a decorating point of view than flowering plants, which are airier in looks. The lush, bold effect of greenery can only be obtained with foliage plants. Also, most flowering plants do not flower all year long. They are in bloom only a few weeks a year, and when they are "resting" they are not always very attractive.

Light indoors is affected by what is outside the window. If your view is unobstructed, maximum sun will come in. If you face the wall of the next building—it's a whole different story. *Without anything in the way,* you could expect the following from these various exposures: East, morning sun but shaded from afternoon sun by your own building. West, no morning sun but long afternoon sun. North, only morning sun. South, early morning sun and late afternoon sun as well. Most city dwellers and suburbanites have windows facing some structure nearby, so use this guide in context with your own location.

Once you have determined which plants are best suited for your light situation, it's up to you which of these you select, since much depends on the effect you wish to achieve. Select from the Specimen List if you're looking for a single dramatic accent in the room. Until they are fully mature and impressive-looking, most of these specimen plants could also be listed on the Foliage List. For example, the Norfolk Island pine can be only eight inches high. Tucked in among other plants, it's an attractive and very different-looking foliage plant. At its maturity, when it's around four feet high, it's one of the handsomest accent plants. But not all foliage plants grow into goodlooking specimens, which is why I made a separate listing of them. To avoid duplication, I did not repeat Specimen under Foliage Plants.

Reference to how much water to give plants mainly covers two instructions: "keep evenly moist" and "water when soil dries out." The latter means that when you stick your finger in the soil, if the soil is really dry and powdery, *then,* you water. In the case of the first, your finger feels moisture *halfway down* the pot. This type of plant does not like to go bone dry before being watered again.

If you're ever in doubt, simply wait another day or two. It's far better to err on the side of not giving enough water than of giving too much. After a while you'll get to know your plants and their needs.

HOW TO SELECT PLANTS

It's obvious but keep it in mind anyway: Buy from a reputable local dealer, somebody who was in business yesterday and will be there again tomorrow. Be prepared to take your risks with people in temporary quarters or selling from a truck parked at the street corner. If something goes wrong with your expensive specimen plant, they may not be around next week to do something about it. Supermarkets and variety stores are not as bad as some make them out to be, for the good reason that they mostly stick to selling hardy varieties that are quite undemanding. I have bought philodendron and ivy from these sources and have not been disappointed.

Although I have tried to stay away from hard-to-find plants, it may be that your local plantsmen do not have the particular variety that you want. In this case, do not hesitate to purchase it from a good mail order firm that specializes in plants. Packaging and shipping are so improved today that you need have no fear of losses, and if there is any trouble, most firms will refund your money if you return the plant within a certain period of time. I purchased a superb, mature spathiphyllum through the mail and it's one of my handsomest plants. It bloomed within two weeks of arrival. However, if at all possible, do buy locally. You'll be able to see exactly what you're getting from a decorating point of view. Since you have a special place in your home in mind when buying the plant, it's best to see it to get the desired effect, as with a piece of furniture. Height, width and shape of plant all play an important part, and they are unknown when you buy by mail—especially for the beginner-gardener who is not yet knowledgeable in the growth habits of plants.

You can usually tell if the plant you're buying is healthy by checking to see if it has new growth. Select those that show new leaves coming out. If it's a flowering plant in bloom, buy one that also has unopened buds. Stick with stocky, bushy plants as opposed to tall, spindly ones—unless that's the way the plant grows normally. Look for any obvious signs of pests or disease. Shrivelled leaves and leaves with holes or with spots are best left alone. The places to look for bugs are under the leaves and where the leaf and stem join. Leaves should have a healthy glow about them; a freshness which you recognize in vegetables when picked fresh as opposed to being on a counter for days. Don't be fooled by excessively shiny leaves—that's not nature. That's a wax spray which some dealers unfortunately use on their plants to give them "glamor" appeal. That one coat won't harm them, but don't repeat the process when you get the plant home. The leaves need to breathe without having their pores clogged.

Important: Repot the plant when you get home, no matter where you bought it. (See Potting under "Culture Requirements.") Mysterious plant deaths have been attributed to all sorts of causes by distressed plant owners, when actually the trouble was improper potting, without adequate drainage at the bottom, and/or a poor soil mixture. I have bought plants from all types of dealers, from top nurserymen to variety stores, and I have been amazed to see how frequently drainage material is missing. In a very tiny pot, this doesn't matter, but in anything over two inches, it becomes vital. In the case of large tubs, obviously repotting is not possible in an apartment. In this case be sure to mention drainage material to the dealer. Better still, buy the container you want in his shop and have him pot the plant in front of you. Simply see that he spreads a layer of broken shard (broken pieces of clay—usually old clay pots that have been sterilized before breaking up) or pebbles or small stones. The larger the pot, the thicker the layer of drainage material should be. In a fourteen-inch pot, I put a layer about two inches deep. When repotting a smaller plant yourself, you can use the pot it came in if you first soak it in water to which you've added some household bleach. Rinse it, dry and you're set to reuse the pot.

The listing of plants is in alphabetical order of their botanical names, but the lists that follow are for those who wish to know at a glance which of these plants are suited to specific light requirements. Some plants do not have common names.

TOLERATING LOW LIGHT

(It should be noted that many of these plants will do better in a low-to-medium light location. Healthy, vigorous growth needs a certain amount of good light; however, these plants can be expected to hold their own in low light.)

Aglaonema (Chinese evergreen)

Araucaria excelsa (Norfolk Island pine)

Asparagus sprengeri (asparagus fern)

Aspidistra elatior (cast iron plant)

Asplenium nidus (bird's-nest fern)

Aucuba japonica variegata (gold-dust tree)

Begonia (rex)

Chamaedorea elegans (Neanthe Bella palm)

Chamaedorea erumpens (bamboo palm)

Cissus rhombifolia (grape ivy)

Collinia elegans bella (dwarf palm)

Cyperus diffusus (umbrella plant)

Dieffenbachia picta (dumbcane)

Dracaena deremensis

Dracaena godseffiana

Dracaena marginata

Ficus carica (fig tree)

Ficus elastica decora (rubber plant)

Ficus lyrata, F. pandurata (fiddle-leaf fig)

Fittonia verschaffeltii

Hedera helix (English ivy)

Howea forsteriana (Kentia palm)

Maranta leuconeura (prayer plant)

Nephrolepis exaltata bostoniensis (Boston fern)

Peperomia

Peperomia prostrata (hanging peperomia)

Philodendron cannifolium (self-heading philodendron)

Philodendron hastatum (hanging philodendron)

Philodendron mcneilianum (self-heading philodendron)

Philodendron oxycardium (*cordatum*) (hanging philodendron)

Philodendron wendlandii (self-heading philodendron)

Plectranthus australis (Swedish ivy)

Podocarpus macrophylla maki

Sansevieria (snake-plant)

Schefflera actinophylla

Scindapsus aureus (pothos)

Spathiphyllum

Tolmiea menziesii (piggy-back plant)

REQUIRING MEDIUM LIGHT

(Some of these plants will do better in the medium-to-bright light areas, especially flowering types.)

Aphelandra (zebra plant)

Begonia, rhizomatous and angel-wing

Begonia semperflorens (wax begonia)

Beloperone guttata (shrimp plant)

Bromeliads

Carissa grandiflora (natal plum)

Chlorophytum elatum (spider plant)

Coleus blumei

Dizygotheca elegantissima (false aralia)

Fatshedera lizei (tree ivy)

Fatsia japonica (aralia)

Saintpaulia (African violet)

Setcreasea purpurea (wandering Jew)

Streptocarpus rexii (cape primrose)

Thumbergia erecta

Zebrina pendula (wandering Jew)

REQUIRING BRIGHT LIGHT

(Plants placed close to window glass need protection from summer noonday sun.)

Abutilon (flowering maple)

Cacti

Cereus peruvianus (cactus)

Codiaeum variegatum (croton)

Gynura aurantiaca (velvet plant)

Hibiscus rosa sinensis (rose-of-China)

Hoya carnosa variegata (wax plant)

Pelargonium hortorum (geranium)

Pelargonium peltatum (ivy geranium)

Sedum morganianum (burro's tail)

Succulents

SPECIMEN PLANTS

Courtesy Everett Conklin and Company, Inc.

Botanical Name:	*ARAUCARIA EXCELSA*
Common Name:	NORFOLK ISLAND PINE
Light Needs:	Low
Soil Mix:	#1
Water:	Keep evenly moist.
Temperature:	Average to cool
Humidity:	Above average preferred
Remarks:	Has a contemporary Christmas-tree look. Can grow to 5 feet.

Courtesy Everett Conklin and Company, Inc.

CEREUS PERUVIANUS

CACTUS

Bright

#3

Water not more than once a week, much less during winter. Wait until soil has thoroughly dried out.

Average to high

Low

Giant, tree-like cactus, much branched. A living sculpture, magnificent in a contemporary room with sunny exposure. Won't flower indoors but the plant is striking enough without blooms. Many other varieties of tall cacti are available.

Courtesy Everett Conklin and Company, Inc.

A-3

CHAMAEDOREA ELEGANS

NEANTHE BELLA PALM

Low

#1

Keep evenly moist.

Average

Average

Where a smaller specimen palm is needed, this is a fine variety. The well-known "Parlor Palm" of yesterday.

Courtesy Everett Conklin and Company, Inc.

Photograph by George Kalmbacher

Botanical Name:	CHAMAEDOREA ERUMPENS	*CYPERUS DIFFUSUS*
Common Name:	BAMBOO PALM	UMBRELLA PLANT
Light Needs:	Low	Low
Soil Mix:	#1	#1
Water:	Keep evenly moist.	Keep wet all the time.
Temperature:	Average	Average to cool
Humidity:	Average	Average
Remarks:	Slow grower. Lush, yet delicate-looking. Other varieties.	This variety is a rapid grower. Other varieties: *alternifolius*, *elegans.*

Courtesy Everett Conklin and Company, Inc.

Courtesy Everett Conklin and Company, Inc.

DIEFFENBACHIA PICTA

DUMBCANE

Low

#1

Water when soil dries out.

Average

Average

Many beautiful varieties available. "Rudolph Rohrs" is a popular one.

DIZYGOTHECA ELEGANTISSIMA

FALSE ARALIA

Medium

#1

Keep evenly moist.

Average

Average to high

Slender, graceful, palm-like leaves

Courtesy Everett Conklin and Company, Inc.

Courtesy Everett Conklin and Company, Inc.

Botanical Name:	*DRACAENA MARGINATA*	*DRACAENA FRAGRANS MASSANGEANA*
Common Name:	DRAGON TREE	CORN PLANT
Light Needs:	Low to medium	Low to medium
Soil Mix:	#1	#1
Water:	Keep evenly moist.	Keep evenly moist.
Temperature:	Average	Average
Humidity:	Average	Average
Remarks:	A favorite with decorators because of its exotic growth habit and dramatic look. Casts fascinating shadows on walls if lighted properly, yet a tough plant for all its glamor.	Bold, striped leaves. If bottom leaves fall, plant a smaller, young Corn Plant at its base to fill out.

Photograph by Brian Manning

Courtesy C. Kind & Co. Inc., New York, N.Y.

FATSHEDERA LIZEI

TREE IVY

Medium

#1

Keep evenly moist at all times.

Average to cool

Average

A hybrid, the result of crossing an ivy with an aralia. Put several plants in one pot for spectacular effect. A handsome plant.

FATSIA JAPONICA

ARALIA

Medium

#1

Keep evenly moist.

Average to cool

Average

Lush-looking plant that grows to large proportions.

Courtesy Everett Conklin and Company, Inc.

Courtesy C. Kind & Co. Inc., New York, N.Y.

Botanical Name:	FICUS CARICA	FICUS ELASTICA DECORA
Common Name:	FIG TREE	RUBBER PLANT
Light Needs:	Low	Low to medium
Soil Mix:	#1	#1
Water:	Keep evenly moist.	When soil dries out.
Temperature:	Average	Average
Humidity:	Average	Average
Remarks:	A favorite with decorators when a delicate look is desired in a traditional room. Variety "Benjamina" has spreading, drooping branches.	A hardy, impressive-looking plant that grows to ceiling if you let it. Good for hot, dry spot. Other good varieties: *doescheri, rubra.*

Courtesy Everett Conklin and Company, Inc.

FICUS LYRATA (OR PANDURATA)

FIDDLE-LEAVED FIG

Low

#1

Keep evenly moist.

Average

Average

Now here's a *big* specimen! Perfect where bold drama is wanted. Not for the timid. Give it plenty of room.

Courtesy Everett Conklin and Company, Inc.

HOWEA FORSTERIANA

KENTIA PALM

Low

#1

Keep evenly moist.

Average

Average

Slow grower. Typical graceful palm look.

Courtesy Rob Herwig

Photographer/Rothschild

Botanical Name:	MONSTERA DELICIOSA	PHILODENDRON McNEILIANUM
Common Name:	SWISS CHEESE PLANT	SELF-HEADING PHILODENDRON
Light Needs:	Low	Low
Soil Mix:	#1	#1
Water:	Keep evenly moist.	Water when soil dries out.
Temperature:	Average	Average
Humidity:	Average	Average
Remarks:	A giant plant, needs plenty of room! Also called *Philodendron pertusum.*	Leaves and stems grow horizontally more than up. Good plant when a low, wide look is desired. Can reach enormous spread. Many other self-heading varieties, some with cut leaves, such as *P. bipinnafidum.*

Courtesy C. Kind & Co. Inc., New York, N.Y.

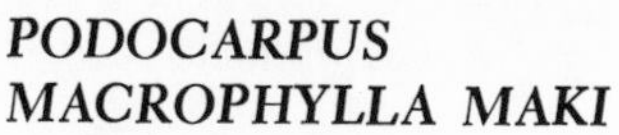

PODOCARPUS MACROPHYLLA MAKI

PODOCARPUS

Low

#1

Keep evenly moist.

Average

Average

Coniferous evergreen, slender leaves. Slow growing. Another good variety: *P. nagi.*

Courtesy Everett Conklin and Company, Inc.

SCHEFFLERA ACTINOPHYLLA

SCHEFFLERA

Low to medium

#1

Water when soil dries out.

Average

Average

A fast-growing, bushy plant. Leaves look like small umbrellas. Many varieties.

FOLIAGE PLANTS

Botanical Name:

Common Name:

Light Needs:

Soil Mix:

Water:

Temperature:

Humidity:

Remarks:

Courtesy Everett Conklin and Company, Inc.

AGLAONEMA

CHINESE EVERGREEN

Low

#1

Keep wet.

Average

Average

A tough plant that likes shady corners. Several varieties.

Courtesy Rob Herwig

ASPIDISTRA ELATIOR

CAST IRON PLANT

Low

#1

Water when soil dries out.

Average

Average

Lives up to its name! A graceful, hardy plant. Variegated varieties.

Photograph by George Kalmbacher

Courtesy C. Kind & Co. Inc., New York, N.Y.

Botanical Name:	ASPLENIUM NIDUS	*AUCUBA JAPONICA VARIEGATA*
Common Name:	BIRD'S-NEST FERN	GOLD-DUST TREE JAPANESE LAUREL
Light Needs:	Low to medium	Low to medium
Soil Mix:	#2	#1
Water:	Keep evenly moist.	Keep evenly moist.
Temperature:	Average to cool	Average to cool
Humidity:	Average	Average
Remarks:	Unlike any other fern in appearance. Large, chartreuse-green leaves. A handsome addition to the indoor garden.	Beautiful leaves speckled with gold. Excellent placed among dark green plants. Compact, slow growth. Prefers unheated rooms like an enclosed porch.

Logee's Greenhouses photograph

Photograph by Brian Manning

BEGONIA REX

BEGONIA

Low to medium

#2

Keep moist at all times.

Average to high

Average to high

These begonias are the types grown primarily for their leaves. Colorful, exotic foliage. Bright hues need more sun than others. Don't plant in too large a pot.

CARISSA GRANDIFLORA NANA COMPACTA

CARISSA

Medium

#1

Keep evenly moist.

Average

Average

Only plant on list which may be hard to locate, but worth the hunt. It's spiny and shrub-like with dark green, glossy, roundish leaves. Unusual branching habit. Makes it good for bonsai. Mine has not needed repotting for five years.

Courtesy Geo. W. Park Seed Co., Inc.

Photograph by Brian Manning

Botanical Name:	*CODIAEUM VARIEGATUM*	*COLEUS BLUMEI*
Common Name:	CROTON	COLEUS
Light Needs:	Bright	Medium to bright
Soil Mix:	#1	#1
Water:	Keep evenly moist.	Keep evenly moist.
Temperature:	Average to high	Average
Humidity:	Average to high	Average
Remarks:	No two leaves are ever the same color on one plant! Numerous varieties.	Brilliantly colored leaves. Pick off flowers for better leaf development. (Flower spikes are not all that great anyway.) Keep pruning plant to avoid legginess.

Photograph by Brian Manning

Courtesy Everett Conklin and Company, Inc.

COLLINIA ELEGANS BELLA

DWARF PALM

Low

#1

Keep evenly moist.

Average

Average

Indispensable for a graceful, airy touch in a grouping of several small foliage plants. A very, very slow grower. Great for dish gardens.

DRACAENA DEREMENSIS

DRACAENA

Low

#1

Keep evenly moist.

Average

Average

Green and white striped leaves. Bushy but not tall. Very lush looking. Many varieties in the dracaena family.

Photograph by Brian Manning

Photograph by George Kalmbacher

Botanical Name:	DRACAENA GODSEFFIANA	*FITTONIA VERSCHAFFELTII*
Common Name:	DRACAENA	FITTONIA
Light Needs:	Low to medium	Low
Soil Mix:	#1	#1
Water:	Keep evenly moist.	Keep evenly moist.
Temperature:	Average	Average to high
Humidity:	Average	Average
Remarks:	Does not resemble any of the usual dracaenas. Shrubby, tough and good-looking. It's a "must" in my home.	A trailing plant to use when you want to hide nearby pots, or to cascade from the edge of a tall planter. Mix with philodendron, ivy or "Pothos" for a trailing "wall" in front of upright plants. Dark green leaves veined with white or pink.

Photograph by Brian Manning

MARANTA LEUCONEURA

PRAYER PLANT

Low to medium

#1

Keep evenly moist.

Average

Average

Handsome striped or blotched leaves. Several varieties. Compact growth habit.

Courtesy Everett Conklin and Company, Inc.

PEPEROMIA

PEPEROMIA

Low to medium

#1

Water when soil dries out.

Average

Average

Undemanding, hardy plants. Many varieties available. They add a different texture to the foliage garden.

Courtesy Rob Herwig

Photograph by Brian Manning

Botanical Name:	*POLYPODIUM AUREUM*	*SANSEVIERIA*
Common Name:	BEAR'S-PAW FERN HARE'S-PAW FERN	SNAKE PLANT MOTHER-IN-LAW TONGUE
Light Needs:	Medium	Low
Soil Mix:	#2	#1
Water:	Keep moist at all times.	Water when soil dries out.
Temperature:	Average	Average
Humidity:	Average	Average
Remarks:	These large ferns make a dramatic impact on the indoor garden. Several varieties available. Same culture as the Boston ferns, so they can be combined.	This plant deserves a better name and better care than it generally receives. Because it's undemanding, it's usually neglected. Its tall, sword-like leaves give contrast to indoor gardens. Several varieties.

Photograph by Brian Manning

TOLMIEA MENZIESII

PIGGY-BACK PLANT

Medium

#1

Keep evenly moist.

Average to cool

Average

Aptly named because new plants grow on top of old leaves. Bright green color. Can qualify as a hanging plant when fully mature.

FLOWERING PLANTS

Photograph by George Kalmbacher

Botanical Name:	*ABUTILON*
Common Name:	FLOWERING MAPLE
Light Needs:	Bright
Soil Mix:	#2
Water:	Keep evenly moist.
Temperature:	Average
Humidity:	Average
Remarks:	Prune in early fall for winter flowers. Hollyhock-type blooms. Several varieties. White, yellow, pink or red flowers.

Courtesy C. Kind & Co. Inc., New York, N.Y.

Merry Gardens photograph

APHELANDRA

ZEBRA PLANT

Medium

#3

Keep evenly moist.

Average

Average

As striking of foliage as of flowers, which are long-lasting. Several varieties. Yellow or orange flowers.

BEGONIA SEMPERFLORENS

WAX BEGONIA

Medium

#2

Keep evenly moist. Do not spray foliage.

Average to warm

Average

Countless species and varieties. No indoor gardener should be without a few. Fibrous-rooted begonias are best for flowering purposes. New hybrid, "Rieger elatior," is a real beauty. White, pink or red flowers.

Merry Gardens photograph

Merry Gardens photograph

Botanical Name:	*BELOPERONE GUTTATA*	*CRASSULACEAE ECHEVERIA, KALANCHOE, LAMPRANTHUS*
Common Name:	SHRIMP PLANT	SUCCULENTS
Light Needs:	Medium to bright	Medium to bright
Soil Mix:	#1	#3
Water:	Water when soil dries out.	Water when soil dries out.
Temperature:	Average to warm	Average
Humidity:	Average	Average
Remarks:	Unusual-looking plant with shrimp-like flowers. Blooms well in a spot that gets good light. Keep pruning to maintain compact growth. Tiny white flowers with shrimp-colored bracts.	As with cacti, there are countless succulents to choose from. They vary in shapes, growth habits and types of blooms, but all are rewarding. White, pink, lavender and red flowers.

Courtesy Everett Conklin and Company, Inc.

BROMELIACEAE
1. *AECHMEA*, 2. *BILLBERGIA*, 3. *CRYPTANTHUS*

BROMELIADS

Will tolerate low light, but need bright to bloom

1. Equal parts osmunda fiber and peat moss plus a bit of sand.
2. Same as above but add pieces of charcoal.
3. Equal parts of loam, sand, peat moss and leaf mold.

1. Water roots sparingly but keep center cup (formed by leaves) filled with water.
2. Same as above, but reduce amount of watering during winter and when in bloom.
3. Water roots sparingly but sprinkle leaves frequently.

Average to warm

Average

The most exotic-looking of flowering house plants. Many varieties within each of the 3 genera listed here. Flowers can last several months, after which plant dies slowly, but new ones sprout at the base. Cut off new sprouts, pot them and start all over again! Grow them on branches to make "plant mobiles." Most roots grow along the surface rather than straight down, so plant in wide shallow pots. Brilliant flowers of all colors. Leaves are also handsomely colored with interesting markings, especially those of *cryptanthus*, which are usually grown for their foliage and should be potted in a shallow container.

Courtesy Geo. W. Park Seed Co., Inc.

Botanical Name: CACTACEAE
ECHINOCEREUS, ECHINOPSIS, EPHIPHYLLUM, GYMNOCALYCIUM, MAMALLARIA, NOTOCACTUS, SCHLUMBERGERA

Common Name: CACTI
HEDGEHOG CACTUS, EASTER LILY CACTUS, ORCHID CACTUS, BARREL CACTUS, LONG LADY FINGER, BALL CACTUS, CHRISTMAS CACTUS

Light Needs: Medium to bright

Soil Mix: #3, except for *ephiphyllum* and *schlumbergera*, where #2 is required

Water: Water when soil is dried out, about every 10 days or so.

Temperature: Average

Humidity: Average to low

Remarks: Fabulous flowers, mostly during summer months. Many genera, species and varieties, but those listed here are among most popular and easy to obtain. Pot cacti only in unglazed containers with drainage holes. Flowers come in all colors except blue.

Courtesy Rob Herwig

HIBISCUS ROSA SINENSIS

HIBISCUS ROSE-OF-CHINA

Bright

#2

Keep evenly moist.

Average

Average

An attractive shrub for a sunny window or a glass wall. Keep pruning to keep it in bloom and within reasonable size. Yellow, pink, red, salmon and white flowers.

Courtesy Geo. W. Park Seed Co., Inc.

PELARGONIUM HORTORUM

GERANIUM

Bright

#1

Water only when soil dries out.

Average

Average

Contrary to popular opinion, this is not a plant to take for granted. Expect flowers chiefly in spring and summer. Stay away from scented and fancy "Lady Washington" varieties— too difficult to grow. White, pink, salmon, red and lavender flowers.

Courtesy Geo. W. Park Seed Co., Inc.

Merry Gardens photograph

Botanical Name:	SAINTPAULIA	*SPATHIPHYLLUM*
Common Name:	AFRICAN VIOLET	SPATHIPHYLLUM "WHITE ANTHURIUM"
Light Needs:	Medium	Low to medium
Soil Mix:	#2	#2
Water:	Keep evenly moist.	Keep moist at all times.
Temperature:	Average	Average to warm
Humidity:	Average to high	Average to high
Remarks:	Easily the most popular flowering house plant, competing with begonias on the number of varieties available! Start with one and you'll end up with ten. Not as difficult to grow as many think or they wouldn't be so popular. White, blue, purple and pink flowers.	One of the handsomest foliage plants, but also bears long-lasting, fragrant white flowers called "spathes." Will take low light, but blooms better in medium. "Mauna Loa" variety is one of my favorite plants.

Photograph by George Kalmbacher

STREPTOCARPUS REXII

CAPE PRIMROSE

Medium

#2

Keep evenly moist.

Average to cool

Average to high

Call it the "Energy Crisis" plant because it prefers cooler rooms, which of course are automatically higher in humidity. Pretty foliage and blue, pink, purple or white flowers.

PLANTS FOR HANGING BASKETS

Courtesy Everett Conklin and Company, Inc.

Botanical Name:	*ASPARAGUS SPRENGERI*
Common Name:	ASPARAGUS FERN
Light Needs:	Low to medium
Soil Mix:	#1
Water:	Keep evenly moist.
Temperature:	Average
Humidity:	Average
Remarks:	Even if you never get to see its tiny fragrant white flowers, followed by brilliant red berries, its light, feathery look is both delicate and lush. I find it absurdly romantic looking and adore it even when it sheds its needles. Mine thrives in very little light.

Merry Gardens photograph

BEGONIA

BEGONIA
ANGEL-WING
RHIZOMATOUS

Medium

#2

Keep evenly moist.

Average

Average

Stay away from the gorgeous but difficult-to-grow tuberous begonias, unless you live in the northwest, or a similar climate. There are many varieties of hanging begonias which are easy to cultivate.

Photograph by Brian Manning

CHLOROPHYTUM ELATUM

SPIDER PLANT

Medium to bright

#1

Keep evenly moist.

Average

Average

A fast grower that quickly outgrows its pot, but may be kept pot-bound for a while, producing flower "babies" (those plantlets that grow at the tip of the long stalks and hang so gracefully). Each plantlet may be cut off and planted separately. The variegated spider plant is more airy and delicate looking, its pale green and white leaves having a fresh, spring-like look.

Courtesy Everett Conklin and Company, Inc.

Photograph by Brian Manning

Botanical Name:	CISSUS RHOMBIFOLIA	GYNURA AURANTIACA
Common Name:	**GRAPE IVY**	**VELVET PLANT**
Light Needs:	**Low to medium**	**Bright**
Soil Mix:	**#1**	**#1**
Water:	**Keep evenly moist.**	**Keep evenly moist.**
Temperature:	**Average**	**Average to high**
Humidity:	**Average**	**Average**
Remarks:	**None better for screening out an undesirable view, forming a dense, lush, full-leaved plant, growing upright as well as hanging. I couldn't do without at least one. It's virtually foolproof. Its relative *Cissus antarctica*, the well-known kangaroo vine, is also very hardy.**	**Snip off flower buds, because the bright orange blooms have a strong, unpleasant odor. A handsome, dramatic-looking plant with brilliant purple leaves which need sun to stay that way.**

Merry Gardens photograph

Merry Gardens photograph

HEDERA HELIX

ENGLISH IVY

Low to medium

#1

Keep evenly moist.

Average to cool

Average

Many varieties! Small-leaved ones are best. Fancy varieties are slower growing, so use in small baskets or plant several to a pot. "Fluffy Ruffles" lives up to its name, a most handsome plant. Mine has done well in both low and bright light.

HOYA CARNOSA VARIEGATA

WAX PLANT

Bright

#1

Water when soil dries out thoroughly.

Average

Average

Buy a mature plant because this is a slow grower, but spectacular when fully grown. Fragrant flowers. Don't remove stems on which flowers grow; those will hold next year's blooms. *Hoya bella* is a miniature-leaved variety.

Courtesy Everett Conklin and Company, Inc.

Courtesy Geo. W. Park Seed Co., Inc.

Botanical Name:	*NEPHROLEPIS EXALTATA BOSTONIENSIS*	*PELARGONIUM PELTATUM*
Common Name:	BOSTON FERN	IVY GERANIUM
Light Needs:	Medium	Bright
Soil Mix:	#2	#1
Water:	Keep moist at all times.	Water when soil dries out.
Temperature:	Average	Average
Humidity:	Average	Average
Remarks:	For a dense but delicate effect, this fern can't be beat. The "conservatory" favorite of the Victorian era. Many varieties, including curly, ruffled ones.	Flowers primarily in summer, but attractive foliage rest of year. For a sunny window. Many colors of blooms.

Merry Gardens photograph

Courtesy Everett Conklin and Company, Inc.

PEPEROMIA PROSTRATA

HANGING PEPEROMIA

Low to medium

#1

Water when soil dries out.

Average

Average

Easy to grow in less sunny areas. Many varieties available. Good for small baskets.

PHILODENDRON OXYCARDIUM (CORDATUM)

P. HASTATUM

PHILODENDRON

Low

#1

Keep evenly moist.

Average

Average

These are the two best varieties for hanging baskets, being smaller-leaved and fuller than their larger relatives. *P. cordatum* is the old standby, not to be scorned simply because it's so undemanding. Excellent for a shady window with a poor view.

Photograph by Brian Manning

Merry Gardens photograph

Botanical Name:	*PLECTRANTHUS AUSTRALIS*	*SCINDAPSUS AUREUS*
Common Name:	SWEDISH IVY	"POTHOS" DEVIL'S IVY
Light Needs:	Low to medium	Low
Soil Mix:	#1	#1
Water:	Keep evenly moist.	Water when soil dries out.
Temperature:	Average	Average
Humidity:	Average	Average
Remarks:	Fresh-green scalloped leaves, attractive branching habit. Beautiful plant even if you never see its flower spikes.	Several varieties, as hardy as philodendron. Falsely called pothos, which doesn't exist in this country.

Merry Gardens photograph

SEDUM MORGANIANUM

BURRO'S-TAIL

Bright

#1

Water when soil dries out.

Average

Average

Makes an exotic-looking basket and a real conversation piece when mature. For a sunny window.

Photograph by Brian Manning

SETCREASEA PURPUREA

WANDERING JEW
PURPLE HEART

Medium

#1

Water when soil dries out.

Average to cool

Average

Fiery purple coloring when getting plenty of sun. Thick, fleshy stems, dainty flowers that nestle inside leaves. Keep pinching for bushy plant.

Photograph by Brian Manning

Botanical Name:	ZEBRINA PENDULA
Common Name:	WANDERING JEW
Light Needs:	Medium
Soil Mix:	#1
Water:	Keep evenly moist.
Temperature:	Average
Humidity:	Average
Remarks:	Can grow to a diameter of several feet. Great plant to team with grape ivy to hide an unsightly view. Keep pinching tips. Most popular variety has purple striped leaves. Very closely related to *Tradescantia. fluminensis variegata,* which has green and white striped leaves.

CARING FOR PLANTS

Which Potting Mixture to Use

A wise precaution which I recommend once again is to repot every plant you buy—regardless of where you purchased it. My personal experience has been that the extra effort is well worthwhile, considering the cost of plants today. Why gamble that a plant will die because it's potted in inadequate soil, or because there is no layer of drainage material at the bottom of the pot? I have had some sad first-hand proof that even top nurseries are careless. And if you buy your plants from one of the no-frills, cut-rate type of places (some of the best sources), you should most definitely repot. Frequently the plant has already outgrown its pot when you buy it. This you can tell when you see roots coming through the drainage hole, or when you take the plant out of its pot and see nothing but a mass of roots tightly curled into a ball. A next-size-larger pot is in order.

There are as many "recipes" for potting mixtures as there are for beef stew, with gardeners insisting on "a pinch of this and a pinch of that" for successful culture of potted plants. The apartment dweller is usually unfamiliar with the various gardening-book terms tossed about with casual abandon, unless he was raised in the country. What exactly is humus? Loam? Leafmold? How can one "cook" without knowing what the ingredients are all about? Some ingredients are interchangeable, and it's good to know which ones.

Loam is regular, good, average garden soil.

Sand refers not to the kind you see on beaches, but to the sharp, coarse builder's sand. It's used to lighten the soil and give it better drainage.

Peat moss, leafmold, humus: These terms probably create the most confusion in the novice gardener's mind. Leafmold and humus are the same thing and can be used interchangeably. Leafmold is peat made of decomposed leaves, twigs and trunks of trees and shrubs. It's very acid when young or "raw," and can burn roots. It's fine when it's older and nearly black in color—the only kind you would be likely to buy already packaged. Peat moss, especially Michigan peat, is less acid than leafmold. There are many kinds of peat, but the one most commonly used for potting mixtures is derived from mosses called sphagnum and from sedges (grasses). Peat moss helps retain moisture in the soil mix. If a potting mixture calls for leafmold (or humus) and you can't get any, simply use peat moss in a higher percentage and you'll be all right.

Limestone is the best form of lime to "sweeten" a soil mixture which otherwise would be too acid for a plant.

Bonemeal is an excellent, slow-acting fertilizer, high in nitrogen and phospheric acid. It can be used safely.

Cow manure. Even the dried variety sold commercially in enormous bags is not recommended for kitchen-counter gardening—which is where most apartment dwellers do their potting of plants. Easy-to-use commercial fertilizers will do an excellent job of keeping your plants in tip-top shape.

The above terms are the ones you will be most likely to come across when house plant soil mixes are discussed. When plants are referred to as "acid loving," as are many begonias, ferns, African violets, gardenias and azaleas, it means that a higher proportion of peat moss is added to the "average" potting mixture. On the opposite side of the scale, anti-acid plants such as cacti and succulents get little or no peat moss in their soil.

Acceptable substitutes. Because of its weight, sand can be a problem for city dwellers. It's heavy to carry home and, when used in hanging baskets, it adds noticeably to the weight which is a factor with certain types of walls and ceilings. I have used perlite most successfully as a sand substitute. The tiny white grains are a silica derivative one-tenth the weight of sand. I can lift a huge bag of it with one hand! I have also tried vermiculite in place of sand, but it retains moisture too well, which, of course, isn't what sand is supposed to do. I find vermiculite great to root seeds and cuttings but I stick with perlite for my potting mixtures.

As already mentioned, when leafmold and/or humus (the same thing) is indicated and you can't get any, substitute regular peat moss instead. Example: If you need two parts loam, one part peat moss and one part leafmold, make it two parts loam and two parts peat moss. Use fish emulsion fertilizer later on to raise and then maintain a high acid content.

When it comes to loam, don't go out and dig in your garden or that of a friend. You'll also dig up all sorts of insects and more trouble than you need to cope with. And besides, the garden soil may be having problems of its own when it comes to a proper balance of various ingredients. It's far better to buy potting soil already packaged. However, don't use it as it comes out of the bag. It needs to be mixed with sand and peat moss. A neat way of storing these ingredients is in covered plastic garbage cans—the large size if you live in a house and have storage room, or the smaller size if you are a cliff dweller. Buy three and use them for potting soil, peat moss and sand (or sand substitute). Use smaller, wastebasket-sized containers for limestone and bone meal. That should take care of your "soil department."

Add a plastic laundry basket to hold pots and saucers, broken shards for use as drainage material, some decorative green sheet moss, fertilizers and pesticides. This completes your garden workshop with minimum of fuss and clutter. If there is no way to hide these plastic containers from view, then simply use attractive covered wicker baskets.

#1 Potting Mixture
(good for almost all house plants):

2 parts loam
1 part peat moss
1 part sand (or perlite)
1 teaspoon bone meal per quart of mixture
1 teaspoon limestone per quart of mixture

Mix all ingredients thoroughly. Many experts like to add ½ part of dried cow manure to this mixture. This is not easy to come by for the average urban gardener, and not pleasant to use. It's best to forget it and fertilize your plants later on. However, gardeners in the country who have a bag of superphosphate handy for other purposes can use this in place of cow manure.

#2 Potting Mixture
(for acid-loving plants):

1 part loam
1 part peat moss
1 part sand (or perlite)
¼ part dried cow manure (or superphosphate, or skip altogether)
1 teaspoon of bone meal per quart of mixture

Mix all ingredients thoroughly.

#3 Potting Mixture
(for most cacti and succulents):

1 part loam
1 part sand (or perlite)
½ part small bits of broken clay pots, broken bricks, or Turface, a coarse processed clay
1 teaspoon of bone meal per quart of mixture
1 teaspoon of limestone per quart of mixture
Mix all ingredients thoroughly.

There are many soilless mixtures which can replace the above three, including the well-known Cornell Peat-Lite Mix, which consists of shredded sphagnum peat moss and perlite, with limestone and various fertilizers added. While this form of gardening—as with growing plants in water—produces equally good results, it is of the utmost importance that fertilizers be regularly applied since nutrients normally found in regular soil are totally lacking in this artificial mixture. For this reason, I only recommend the use of a soilless mixture if weight is a crucial factor in growing indoor plants. For those interested, I suggest writing to Cooperative Extension, New York State College of Agriculture, Cornell University, Ithaca, New York, 14850, for a copy of their bulletin on the Cornell Peat-Lite Mix. Or, write to your local Office of Agricultural Extension Service or the local County Agricultural Agent—both listed in the phone book.

How to Pot a Plant

There is no mystery to potting a plant, simply a few easy steps to follow. First, have the correct soil mixture ready, together with a clean pot. If it's a new clay pot, soak it for a few hours in a bucket of water; since clay absorbs water so readily, it would rob the newly potted plant of moisture. Next, have some clean drainage material handy. This usually consists of broken pieces of old clay pots that have first been soaked in water to which household bleach has been added to kill any trace of disease or insects. Rinse these bits of clay in clear water before using them. Gravel can also be used instead of clay pieces.

Now that you have everything ready, you can start.

1. Gently knock plant out of its present container. This is easily done by tapping the side of the pot against a counter or on the floor. If it's really pot-bound, you may have to push the rubber end of a pencil into the bottom hole to help ease the root ball out. If you're still having a tough time, sacrifice the pot. Break it and gently take the plant out. (It's by breaking these old pots that you accumulate drainage material for repotting.) Remove any old bits of clay that may be embedded in the roots.

2. Place a layer of broken clay bits in the bottom of new pot. The larger the pot, the deeper the layer of drainage should be. A very small pot would only need three or four small pieces. When potting a shrub or tree, cover drainage material with a layer of *coarse* sphagnum moss to prevent soil from seeping into the drainage layer.

3. Depending on size of root ball, fill one-third or one-fourth of the pot with soil mixture.

4. Take the plant and place it in the middle of the pot. Do not push the roots into the soil, but keep adding soil all around the plant until you come to within one inch of the rim of the pot.

5. Press the surface of the soil firmly all around the plant. Do this with your fingers, or, if potting a large tub plant, use a broom handle. Tap the pot gently to settle soil.

6. Water the plant thoroughly until water comes out the bottom hole. Tap the pot again to make sure there are no air pockets. Soil should not come right up to the rim of the pot, as there must be room for water to collect and sink through the roots. Always leave at least an inch between the soil surface and the pot rim.

If you are repotting a plant that you've had for some time, it probably has too many roots and too little soil. The time has come to root-prune it, if you don't wish to go to a size larger pot. Root-pruning is quite simple. Take a very sharp knife (a small saw may be needed for shrubs and trees) and cut one inch off the sides of the root ball, and about one and a half inches off the bottom of the root ball. Repot the plant in its old container with a fresh soil mixture. When this is done, about a third of the top of the plant must be pruned back to compensate for the root pruning. This means cutting back the stems or branches one-third from their tips. Water thoroughly. Do not fertilize root-pruned plants for at least one month afterward. Give the plant time to adjust itself to what is, after all, major surgery. Refusing to go past the fourteen-inch tub it was already in, I drastically cut back an old gardenia, using a hefty saw and all of my strength. The plant not only survived but is thriving! At this rate, I'll have to root-prune it again in a couple of years.

The finishing touch to potting a large plant is a layer of mulch on the surface. It keeps the plant cool in summer and conserves moisture. Also, it looks pretty. The mulch material can be green sheet moss, ornamental stones, gravel, fine-textured redwood or pine bark chips. The last two can also be purchased in nugget form, which is suitable only for large tubs.

In the case of double-potting, mentioned so often in this book, a mulch is essential to hide the inner pot. Use plain (and inexpensive) sphagnum moss between the two pots, adding the costlier green sheet moss on the surface.

How to Water a Plant

This is always a great mystery to novice gardeners. They tend to think that a plant must be watered on specified days, regularly, and in the same manner all year around. "Every three days" or "twice a week" is what they want to hear. This can't be, for many reasons. First, the plant is not thirsty on a clock-like basis, any more than people are. We crave a cool drink more in summer because we're warmer and need it more than we do in December. It's the same with plants. They want water when they need it—*not automatically*. Overwatering is the quickest way to kill plants.

Many factors determine how much and how often a plant needs water:

The *size and type of pot* are important. The smaller the pot, the more quickly the soil inside dries out. Clay is porous and dries out faster than a plastic pot. Wood containers also dry the soil out faster than plastic. Hanging baskets need more frequent watering because they are exposed on all sides to the air currents.

The type of soil matters, too. The more peat moss in it, the more water will be retained. The opposite is true with sand.

Temperature, both indoors and out, affects watering. The cooler the weather, the less water a plant needs. The more the sun shines, the more water is necessary.

The *season* of the year must be considered. Most plants go through a dormancy period during winter. They are not as active and require far less water. It's better to keep them on the dry side. When plants start to grow actively in the spring, their need for moisture increases, especially when they start to flower.

Health is a factor. A vigorous, healthy plant needs adequate water to grow, but one that is ailing due to some disease or pests requires far less. When I notice that a plant suddenly requires little water, I know that something is wrong. I isolate it and almost always find I'm right.

The *size of the root ball* influences watering. The type of plant that grows a massive tangle of roots, such as the mature spider plant, requires plenty of water. This is because little soil is left in the pot, and the water simply drains out in a hurry. Root pruning is in order, but if this isn't done, extra watering is required.

Finally, consider the *type of plant*. This is where personality comes in! As with children, each plant is different, even those of the same variety. It's a mistake to take it for granted that *all* begonias or *all* ivies have to be watered on the same day and in the same amount. There may be one or two in the midst that will surprise you. Some plants are the "lush drinkers" of horticulture, and others have thick, fleshy stems or leaves which make them "camels."

In view of all this, how can one be really sure when a plant needs water? The simplest way of all: Stick your finger in the pot, and feel whether the soil is moist or dry. Your touch will tell you (so will your finger nails). If it's moist, leave the plant alone. If the soil is dry, water it. Pay no attention to when you last watered the plant. Many factors may have come into play to make the plant more or less thirsty than usual. Just go by what your finger tells you. It's the closest thing to a foolproof method as has yet been devised.

After a while, the experienced gardener can tell the degree of dryness by the color of the soil. The darker it is, the more moisture remains. But you have to know what soil mixture you used in the first place if you go by this method—so it's only for those who have learned by experience. If the soil has shriveled away from the inside of the pot, watering is long overdue! The finger test would have prevented this drastic condition.

How to water is as important as when to water. Most people make it harder for themselves with daily sprinklings which do more harm than good. The rule is: *Less often, but thoroughly.* When your finger tells you it's time to water, *keep pouring water in the pot until you see it coming out the bottom hole.* The saucer may overflow if it's too small, so have a pan handy. If only a little water stays in the saucer, leave it there. Evaporation and the extra "drink" that the plant will absorb takes care of it.

One of the reasons for putting gravel at the bottom of the outer pot when double-potting is that if excess water collects, root rot will be avoided because the plant will touch only the gravel, not the water. (See the illustration on page 18.)

Plants don't like ice-cold water, so when you fill the watering can at the sink, turn the hot water faucet for a few seconds, and then fill with cold water. This will make a pleasant, room-temperature liquid.

Ventilation

What's not good for people is generally not good for plants. Don't place them in front of an air conditioner in use, nor in front of a fan. Any drafty location should be avoided. Tops of hot, uncovered radiators are absolutely out unless you want cooked plants as vegetables for dinner. The tops of television sets are very bad for plants (and decor) because of the rays transmitted by the set. What *is* good for plants is any adequate supply of fresh air. If, at certain times of the year, the air is stagnant, provide circulation by turning on a fan—away from the plants—in order to get stale air out and fresh air in. If plants are on a window sill, open the window from the top.

Pruning Plants

Root-pruning has already been discussed (on page 211) and should be done whenever a plant outgrows its pot and you don't want to go into a larger one. This usually happens when a plant has been repotted several times and has at last reached a size beyond which the homeowner does not wish to go unless a new wing is built on the house.

Pruning house plants is done for one of three reasons: shape, health and growth. In the case of shape—as with shrubs outdoors—great care must be exercised. Indoor trees and shrubs may have branches going out in weird directions. Trim them back with very sharp shears to the shape you want, being careful to do it a bit at a time so as not to overdo it. Once a branch is cut, forget it. You can't glue it back on again. Prune to shape only when the overall contour of the plant disturbs you and you feel that a snip here and there will enhance the looks of the plant.

Pruning for health reasons really means cutting out anything that is already dead, damaged or diseased. If a stem has accidentally broken off, cut it neatly back to the juncture of leaf and stem or right down to the base. If one part of the plant looks healthy and vigorous and another is droopy, isolate the plant and immediately cut away what is sickly. (Wash the scissors before using them on another plant to avoid transmitting any disease.)

The frequently-heard term of "pinching back" a plant really describes a form of pruning. All it means is snipping off new tip growth between your thumbnail and forefinger; or, if you've waited too long and the plant has become far too leggy, pinch back an inch or so. Always cut back to an "intersection," where leaf and stem join. The purpose of pinching back a seemingly healthy plant is to keep it bushy at the base. When you think of it, it makes sense. Instead of having to do all that work sending up food and water to the very tips of leggy stems, the plant which has been cut back can concentrate more in the roots, from which new growth will come. Hanging baskets, especially, need regular pinching if they're to be kept full and lush-looking.

Most people are deathly afraid of pruning a plant. They feel they are mutilating them. This sort of overly tender care is the same as that of giving a plant too much water—far from doing good, it can be harmful, if not deadly, for the plant. The worst result of cutting back a little too far is that the plant will simply take a bit longer to fill out, or that you won't have any flowers for a while since you snipped off the buds as they were about to burst. The best time to pinch back is right after a flower has faded. I repeat, *do not be afraid of pinching back a plant*. Use a pair of sharp scissors if the stem is too tough or too large for your fingernails to do the job. Also, it's better to keep pinching back a tiny bit than to wait until you have to chop off a good deal of the plant. Not that this is harmful, but it won't make for a very attractive plant.

Fertilizing Plants

This is another way of saying that you should "feed" your plants from time to time. Since house plants are confined to a small area of soil in which to grow and draw out nutrients, they need outside help, especially during their busy growing season.

As with watering, don't fertilize on a set, routine basis. Here are a few don'ts:

Don't fertilize a sick plant. It needs to make it back to health slowly and gently without the jarring push that fertilizing would give.

Don't fertilize when the plant is dormant, which means during the winter months. When growth slows down and you note that the plant requires less water, don't feed it.

Don't fertilize during cloudy, rainy spells. If it rains for a week or more, put off the feeding.

Don't feed a newly potted plant. Wait a couple of weeks.

The time of year when a plant needs extra food is its most active period, which means spring and summer. Feed it every two or three weeks, slowing down to every four or five weeks during fall, and then hold off until the following spring.

Liquid fertilizers are best for indoor use, for they are the easiest to handle. *Follow manufacturer's directions exactly* when it comes to how much to mix. Too much of the concentrate in proportion to water can burn the roots and kill the plant. Water the plant first, and then fertilize it.

There is no need to turn into a drugstore, with a different fertilizer for each plant. Two should suffice: one for most regular plants, and the other for the more acid-loving ones. For the latter, which include begonias, ferns and gesneriads, I prefer organic fish emulsion—in spite of its unpleasant odor, contrary to claims of having been "deodorized." Fortunately, the odor only lasts while the actual fertilizing is going on, so it isn't all that annoying. I classify a powdered fertilizer under liquid, if it must be mixed with water before applying to a plant. This is as easy to use as the fertilizer which comes in a liquid concentrate.

To make it easy, mark off (with nail polish) on your watering can the level of water at the one quart or half-gallon point. Most fertilizers are geared to one tablespoon per gallon. So figure out what your can holds, put the appropriate amount of fertilizer directly into the can, and fill it up with water. Turn the water faucet on full for a second or so; this will mix the solution with the water.

Grooming Your Plants

People and animals need grooming to look and feel their best, and so do plants. A once-a-week going over is sufficient. On your rounds, carry a pair of sharp scissors, a paper bag, a soft brush and a fine-mist sprayer. Go from plant to plant and:

Pick off any dead leaves.

Pinch back plants that are getting just a tiny bit straggly.

Look for any signs of disease or pests. If you're suspicious, take the plant to the sink and wash off the leaves with soap and water. Isolate it for a week. If you're still in doubt, give the plant a dose of pesticide.

Dust leaves of smooth foliage plants. (Leave hairy leaves alone.) Use a soft brush. Occasionally, wash the leaves with a ball of cotton or a sponge.

Spray a fine mist on foliage plants and humidity-loving plants.

Rotate plants that appear to be doing only so-so. Sometimes there's nothing the matter with them that another location won't fix. A few feet in one direction or another can make a difference. It could be a trifle too sunny this time of year, or too shady—whatever it may be, experiment a bit. Naturally, leave those plants alone which are flourishing where they are.

Nursing Your Plants

Better face it. Anything that is alive may get sick. The first thing to do is to practice preventive medicine. This means buying only healthy plants from a good dealer, potting them correctly in the proper soil, watering them only when they need it, giving them plenty of room and good air circulation, and making a grooming inspection once a week. Following these simple procedures cuts down immensely on the likelihood of a plant becoming diseased, but it still may happen.

So many things can go wrong with a sick plant that whole books could be and have been written about plant pests and diseases (see bibliography). It comes as a surprise to many people that plants can have a disease, internally, besides being prey to the more generally known insects. There are virus diseases, fungus diseases, bacterial diseases and still more! For the average indoor gardener, knowing how to identify and treat these ailments is next to impossible. It's best to destroy the plant (which in some cases is the only control of the disease anyway) or spray it with a fungicide. On the whole, most apartments and houses are so low in humidity that threat of fungus disease is not serious.

It takes a while for a plant to make the adjustment from a florist's shop or the cool moist conditions of a greenhouse where they're grown to their ultimate home, which is hot and dry. It's to be expected that there will be a slight setback, with a few leaves falling. This often distresses the solicitous owner, who thinks a mysterious disease has taken hold of his plant. Keeping the plant a bit on the dry side will help it adjust.

Insect damage is easier to control than internal disease, because the culprits can frequently be seen (a magnifying glass is a good helper to have on hand to help spot those pests that can't be seen by the naked eye). Spider mites, aphids, mealybugs and scales are the most frequently found insects on house plants. Many leave a sticky substance on the leaves, which in turn get a black, sooty covering.

As a *first* measure of control, take the sick plant to the kitchen sink and plunge it, headfirst, into lukewarm soapy water. Cover the soil with aluminum foil so that it doesn't fall into the pan while the pot is being overturned. Swish the leaves around a bit in the solution, and then let stand for about one hour. Rinse under lukewarm water and isolate it for a day or two. If insects return, it's time to use a pesticide. For home use, a spray can is the most convenient. Multi-purpose *house* plant sprays are also available, which kill more than one kind of bug and control fungus disease as well. I repeat a word of caution, which is emphasized because it's so important: *follow manufacturer's directions scrupulously.* If it says "spray plant from a distance of eighteen inches," if need be measure, but make it eighteen inches. It goes without saying that you should never spray near food, pets or people. Some sprays are non-toxic, others aren't. It's a good, safe rule to treat them as though they were *all* toxic. This way you can't forget to be cautious as you switch from one to the other.

Besides washing in soapy water, the old standby of dipping a Q-Tip in alcohol and applying it to the backs of leaves is good for sucking insects like aphids and mealybugs. Several applications may be necessary, but it's effective.

Last but not least: *Control* is what you're after, not eradication. There will always be bugs with us. They multiply so rapidly, and with such gusto, that all we can do is keep down their population in the home. Good plant housekeeping—meaning the weekly grooming bit and regular washing of plants, plus a prompt attack on the culprits—should keep the damage under control. If not, then bite your lip and throw the plant out.

MOST COMMON HOUSE PLANT PESTS AND DISEASES

Name	*Description*	*Control*
Aphids	Sucking insects with soft bodies, sometimes called plant lice. Many kinds and colors. Usually cluster around new growth and buds.	Use house-plant spray containing malathion.

Name	*Description*	*Control*
Cyclamen Mites	Invisible to the naked eye. They attack young parts of the plant. Buds get deformed, leaves curl and wrinkle. Highly contagious to other plants.	Use special miticide spray made for mites.
Mealybugs	They look like little balls of cotton; are actually soft-bodied sucking insects.	Remove with cotton swabs dipped in alcohol or nail polish remover, or use spray containing malathion as last resort.
Red Spider Mites	Invisible to the naked eye until they've increased, then you see fine cobwebs between leaves and stems. Leaves finally look like transparent lace.	Use special miticide spray made for mites.
Scales	There are many kinds of these sucking insects, usually brown or gray, with soft or hard shells.	Use spray containing malathion.
Whiteflies	These pests have tiny white wings and are found on the undersides of leaves. Can form a cloud above plant when leaves are disturbed. They suck juices from the leaves, turning them yellow, and excrete a sticky substance which turns into sooty mold.	Until recently malathion was best control. Now, use spray containing the synthetic pyrethroid, Resmethrin. Repeat treatment frequently to undersides of leaves, as these flies multiply rapidly and in large numbers.

Fungus, Bacterial and Virus Diseases. Fortunately, house plants are seldom affected by diseases, which require experience and skill to treat correctly. Among these are leaf blotch, damping-off, leaf spot, root rot, stem rot, crown rot, rust and mildew. For some there is no control yet known; for others, picking off and burning the affected leaves is the first step, followed by an application of fungicide such as benomyl or a Bordeaux mixture. Isolate plant and discard promptly if it doesn't respond to treatment. If you're sure a pest is not the culprit, my advice is to forget the plant. If it's a valuable one, take it to a knowledgeable local plantsman or your city botanical garden.

IMPORTANT NOTE: All ferns are highly sensitive to malathion, so do not spray them with anything containing this insecticide. Instead, use nicotine sulfate and soap.

Plant Propagation

This scares away the novice gardener like nothing else, except possibly pruning. For the purposes of this book, all we are interested in is how to increase our collection of plants in the most elementary manner without taking extensive gardening courses. Cuttings are the answer. It's ridiculously easy. A warm, moist atmosphere is all you have to contribute, since the closer you can duplicate a greenhouse atmosphere, the faster the cutting will grow.

I find the principle of double-potting best—even in my greenhouse—because it solves the tricky problem of watering. The propagation medium should be kept constantly moist, but not wet, and this is done automatically in double-potting, as the medium keeps drawing just the same amount of water it needs.

You will need the following: one large pan (either buy a plastic one made for the purpose from your plant shop, or use a large Pyrex baking pan), and several small clay pots or a large clay bulb pan. (If you ever buy nursery plants in those small, squarish plastic boxes with holes at the bottom, save them. They're marvelous for rooting cuttings. Six of these small pans fit into the standard larger one.) You'll then need vermiculite (this is a sterile medium which I've found excellent, used alone, for rooting most cuttings—small bags are available at garden centers), hormone rooting powder (like Rootone; this isn't a must, but I like to use it in order to prevent the possibility of any root rot, and it helps to promote growth), and paper towels.

Now here's all you do: **1.** Put a layer of paper towel at the bottom of a clay pot or small plastic box. This is to prevent the vermiculite from falling out the drainage holes. **2.** Fill pot with vermiculite; wet thoroughly. **3.** Take the cutting and dip it in hormone powder. With a pencil or similar object, make a hole in the wet vermiculite. Insert the cutting into the hole, and press firmly all around it with your fingers. **4.** Place the pot or pan inside the larger pan. **5.** Add about one inch of water to large pan. The vermiculite will keep drawing up water as it needs it. Always keep some water at the bottom of the larger pan for this reason, since it's vital that the cutting never be allowed to dry out.

After ten days or so, gently tug at the cutting, trying to lift it out. If it slips out easily, press it back into the vermiculite. It hasn't yet got enough roots. When it has a sufficient number, you will note that it's difficult to lift out the cutting. This means the roots are hanging on to the rooting medium. Take a tablespoon and lift the entire root mass. It may be just a little, or it may be an enormous ball of roots clinging to a lot of vermiculite. All the better. Have a clean small pot ready with the appropriate soil (1 part loam, 1 part sand or perlite, and 1 part peat moss, with a pinch of limestone added), and plant the rooted cutting very gently. Water with care so as not to injure the tiny plant. Keep it evenly moist as it keeps growing.

Basically, this is all there is to rooting cuttings. Experience is the best teacher. After doing this a while, the indoor gardener develops a "feel" for it. Instinctively he'll know, for instance, not to place the rooting pan in sunlight because this would burn the cutting. Even after the young plant has been potted, it should be kept in bright light, but not in direct sun, for a couple of weeks.

Many people argue that it's much easier to root cuttings directly in water. This may be true, but it's also a greater risk. The new plant has developed roots that have adapted themselves to a water environment; when they are eventually transferred to soil the shock sometimes kills the plant, or it takes a long time to get established. This is a gamble the gardener has to take. If the plant is to be kept permanently in water, obviously there is no problem.

The actual taking of the cutting is also quite simple. With a sharp knife or scissors, snip off the growing tip of a plant, about two inches of it. Leave only several top leaves, taking off those that may grow along the rest of the stem. If there's a bud or a faded flower, snip it off, too. If, as happens frequently, the cutting starts to bloom while still making roots in the vermiculite, cut off the flowers. The reason for this is that all the energy the plant has should go towards making roots, not flowering. One would be done at the expense of the other.

There are many other ways one can propagate a plant. African violets and rex begonias are done from a single leaf. In the case of the first, a one-inch stem is left on the leaf and inserted in the rooting medium. As for the latter, several slashes of the "veins" on the back of the fleshy leaf will produce roots if the leaf has its back kept pressed against the moist vermiculite.

If the little "baby spiders" are cut off from the long stems connecting them to the mother plant, new spider plants are thus propagated. The roots are already formed, and need only be activated in moist vermiculite for a week or so. The huge root mass which develops can be transplanted to a pot.

I suggest that the novice gardener begin with these easy methods of propagating before tackling more difficult ones, such as air-layering and tuber divisions. Growing from seed requires constant attention and care and is not as immediately rewarding as growing from a cutting.

Humidity is an important factor in propagation. For this reason, it may be a good idea to cover your cuttings with a plastic "bubble." Bend a wire coat hanger and form a couple of "ribs" over the pan. Cover this with clear plastic. Punch a few holes in the plastic to prevent too much humidity and possible rot.

Since it takes a while for a rooted cutting to develop into a handsome show plant, try to set aside a tiny space in your house for your "nursery." Here you can set up the propagation pan filled with cuttings, and the few pots of young, newly rooted plants. You can have a perpetual source of certain "stock" items in this manner, if you take cuttings regularly. The dear old standbys such as ivies, philodendrons, wandering Jews, wax begonias and others can always be readily available when replacement is in order.

Summer Care

If you live in an apartment, you need not concern yourself with summer care of your plants. Leave them where they are and they'll do well. If you have a terrace, *make sure that it's protected* before you bring out any plants. The wind can do fatal damage to plants. Put plants on the floor, in a corner which is sheltered from breezes and from intense sun.

It's a different story for house dwellers. They have a choice of leaving the plants indoors or bringing them outside. Since we are concerned with plants grown primarily for decorating purposes, the owner must decide whether or not he wishes to leave "holes" throughout the house during the summer months in order to give his plants a vacation in the great outdoors. Also, much depends on whether or not he needs the extra plants outdoors. Perhaps he already has large containers on the terrace filled with annuals which serve the purpose of bringing flowers and color to the outdoor entertaining area.

Large specimen plants in heavy tubs obviously cannot and shouldn't be moved. Neither should any prized plant which would be hard to replace. It should be remembered that once outdoors, plants are at the mercy of the elements. Hard rain, fierce winds, animals—all take their toll on plants, unless one is on the scene at all times, and wishes to keep bringing in plants at a moment's notice, even in the middle of the night!

If you rearrange the interior decoration of your home during the summer months, and you decide to bring some plants outdoors, here are some suggestions:

In general, stick to the same light requirements outdoors that a plant needs indoors. If a plant doesn't like sun inside, it's not going to like it outside where it's far more intense. No plant likes wind, so select a sheltered spot on the terrace for sun-loving plants and put those preferring shade under a tree. If your terrace area has an awning, this is an excellent spot for those plants not requiring full sun. I keep many of my plants under an awning, grouping the most sun-loving ones near the edge, and the others well under. Make sure that they are not at the very edge, however, or they will get drenched by the water pouring down the sides when it rains.

Keep all the plants in their own pots. Group them together for best effect (the same principle that holds true for indoors works for outdoors as well) and for ease of watering and grooming. Follow the same procedures that you would indoors. Unless there is rain, water plants as needed. Those under awnings and in heavily sheltered areas should be checked frequently, since rain never touches them.

Hang baskets under a tree, from lower branches. They will make a handsome "hanging garden." Baskets generally dry out faster, but especially outdoors when the wind dehydrates the soil quickly. Check for watering often.

Don't make a rapid transition from the cozy indoor environment to the hazardous outdoors. Put the plants in a "decompression chamber" such as a garage or a porch. The idea is to harden them, toughening them up for the harsher conditions outside. Do this for a week, and then set them where you want them. Make sure you know the date of the usual last frost in your area. You probably do already if you live in colder areas; if not, ask your local Agricultural Agent or garden center. Play safe. Don't rush the season simply because spring has suddenly gone into summer temperatures. It may go way down the next day.

When the time comes to bring the plants back indoors, be just as cautious about the weather. Get them inside before any risk of early frost. Check them thoroughly for insects, damage, or roots growing through the drainage hole indicating a need for repotting or root pruning (see page 211). No need for any decompression treatment, since they're going into a controlled, favorable environment.

Vacation Care

If a few steps are followed, plants can be left to fend for themselves indoors for a period of up to two weeks, but not longer. For long absences, arrangements should be made with a friend or neighbor, or with a local florist who will tend your plants for a small fee.

Don't leave any house plants outdoors. Sudden storms and heavy rains could kill them. Sheltered porches are fine since plants are not left to the mercy of the elements. But don't leave them on tables. Put them on the floor of the porch near the wall of the house. A corner is the best location. Have a friend come in to water them.

For plants kept indoors, first thoroughly water them. Then place a thick layer of newspapers at the bottom of your bathtub. Turn on the water and soak the newspapers. Put the plants on top of the papers. Form a *clear* plastic cover over the plants with dry-cleaner bags or a drop cloth from a hardware store. Hold the cover away from the plants by spreading it on a laundry rack or a step ladder. Use any device that will keep the plastic above and on the sides of the plants without touching them. Tuck the plastic under newspapers and punch a few holes for ventilation. Leave the bathroom lights on.

Plants can be individually protected by putting a couple of stakes in the pot and wrapping plant and pot in clear plastic. Make sure the plant is watered first. Where plants are double-potted, thoroughly wet the sphagnum moss between the two pots. The moisture will seep through the walls of the porous inner pot and keep the plant happy. Always punch a few holes for ventilation.

It's important to keep plants out of direct sunlight. This dries out the soil in no time, and when you're away you have no control over watering. Temporarily move the plants away from a sunny window to a shadier spot; otherwise the plants will not only be dehydrated but will cook inside their plastic bubbles. If you have translucent window shades which screen out the sun rays but allow light in, pull them down for the duration of your trip. It's a good idea to do this, even when you're home, during the hottest days of summer when the afternoon sun is strongest.

Obviously you can't move or wrap up large specimen plants. On the other hand, because they're in large tubs, these don't dry out as fast. They should be set on pebbles in saucers, or else be double-potted with the inner pot sitting on pebbles. Water the plant thoroughly, allowing the water that drains out to cover the pebbles. Add more water if there is not enough. The idea is to leave the plant on a bed of moistened pebbles which will keep it sufficiently watered until your return.

If large pots are mulched—as they should be—this too keeps the moisture in the soil. Remember that more plants are lost from overwatering than from underwatering. Even if plants appear wilted on your return, a thorough soaking will revive them. Also keep in mind that the smaller the pot, the more quickly the soil dries out, and that plastic pots keep moisture in longer than do clay pots. If you're a frequent traveler, it might be best for you to concentrate on larger plants in plastic pots, which in turn are placed inside ornamental waterproof containers.

SUPPLIERS OF PLANTS AND ACCESSORIES

NOTE: Many of the nurseries I have listed carry additional plants besides those mentioned, but I stressed those plants which would be of greatest interest to the readers of this book. Most nurseries have catalogs—some free—which tell you exactly what plant material and accessories they have.

My recommendation is to scout your local plant shops first and buy the sturdy foliage plants which form the backbone of indoor gardens. You'll be able to obtain just the size plant you need and see exactly how it will fit into your decorating scheme. Local shops usually stock the kinds of plants that do well under typical apartment conditions.

Unless your own particular locality is fortunate enough to have garden supply centers with a good selection of bromeliads, begonias, cacti, succulents, and so forth, this is where the mail order nursery comes to the rescue. It sells plants that usually can't be obtained locally—some rare and for the really experienced gardener; others not rare, but hard to get in one's own neighborhood.

The ingredients for potting mixtures are usually available locally (packaged potting soil, peat moss, sand or perlite, etc.) but in case they aren't, there are nurseries that will send these to you. Supplies for gardening under artificial lights are frequently very hard to obtain, so do send for the catalogs of the firms I have listed. Specialties such as aquatic gardening, terrariums or bonsai also require plants not commonly available except through mail order.

Don't be afraid of ordering by mail. Nurserymen are expert horticulturists and use the latest methods of shipping plant material so as to have it arrive in excellent condition. Unless you so specify, most plants are young, therefore small. They'll grow into the large, full plants you expect if you give them the care they need. The experienced gardener knows the potential of a plant and is not shocked at the sight of a comparatively scrawny-looking thing. He knows what it will look like a year later. If you're a house dweller and have the room, allow these smaller plants to mature by themselves, and then bring them into the living room or other areas where you have indoor gardens on display.

A final word of advice to beginners: Start cautiously. Buy easy-to-grow and easy-to-obtain-locally plants and get the feel of caring for them and displaying them effectively. *Then,* after glorious results that bolster your morale, send for the more exciting varieties. Your increasing self-confidence will see you through the new adventure!

A. L. Randall Company
1325 West Randolph Street
Chicago, Ill. 60607

Containers.

Abbey Garden
P.O. Box 167
Reseda, Calif. 91335

Cacti and succulents.

Albert H. Buell
Eastford, Conn. 06242

African violets and gesneriads.

Alberts & Merkel Bros. Inc.
2210 S. Federal Highway
Boynton Beach, Fla. 33435

Specimen and foliage plants, ferns.

Antonelli Brothers
2545 Capitola Rd.
Santa Cruz, Calif. 95060

Gesneriads, gloxinias.

Architectural Pottery
P.O. Box 34847
2020 S. Robertson Blvd.
Los Angeles, Calif. 90034

Containers.

Artemide
1345 Avenue of the Americas
New York, N.Y. 10019

Containers.

Arthur Eames Allgrove
North Wilmington, Mass. 01887

Ferns, sheet moss, terrarium and bonsai plants and supplies.

Bernard D. Greerson 3548 N. Cramer Street Milwaukee, Wis. 53211	*Fertilizers, soil mixes, etc.*
Burgess Seed & Plant Co. Galesburg, Mich. 49053	*Dwarf citrus and house plants.*
Cactus Gem Nursery P.O. Box 327 Aromas, Calif. 95004	*Cacti and succulents.*
Cook's Geranium Nursery 712 North Grand Lyons, Kan. 67554	*All kinds of geraniums.*
De Jager, P. and Sons, Inc. South Hamilton, Mass. 01982	*Bulbs for forcing.*
Denver Terra Cotta Co. 135 Tejon Street Denver, Colo. 80202	*Containers.*
Edelweiss Gardens 54 Robbinsville-Allentown Rd. Robbinsville, N.J. 08691	*Ferns and terrarium plants.*
Elon, Inc. 964 Third Avenue New York, N.Y. 10022	*Containers made of decorative tiles.*
Everett Conklin and Company, Inc. Montvale, N.J. 07645	*Specialists in indoor and outdoor plantings for offices and industry.*
Featherock, Inc. 2890 Empire P.O. Box 6190 Burbank, Calif. 91510	*Featherock for indoor gardens, terrariums, bonsai. Write for list of distributors in your area.*
Fischer Greenhouses Lindwood, N.J. 08221	*African violets and gesneriads.*

Fleco Industries 3347 Halifax Street Dallas, Tex. 75247	*Artificial lighting fixtures.*
Fran's Basket House Route 10 Succasunna, N.J. 07876	*Wicker and rattan trays, baskets, planters.*
George W. Park Seed Co., Inc. Greenwood, S.C. 29646	*Seeds for house plants, equipment and supplies.*
Gilmore Plant & Bulb Co., Inc. Julian, N.C. 27283	*Trees, shrubs, vines.*
Girard Nurseries Geneva, Ohio 44041	*Bonsai plants and supplies.*
Green House, The 9515 Flower Street Bellflower, Calif. 90706	*Fertilizers, soil mixes, etc.*
Habitat 341 East 62nd Street New York, N.Y. 10021	*Containers.*
Helen O'Hara 1 Darby Place Glen Head, N.Y. 11545	*Cacti and succulents, and Featherock supplies.*
Henrietta's Nursery 1345 N. Brawley Fresno, Calif. 93705	*Cacti and succulents.*
Hilltop Herb Farm Box 866 Cleveland, Tex. 77327	*Herbs, geraniums.*
House Plant Corner, The Box 165 Oxford, Md. 21654	*All kinds of house plants and supplies, including those for artificial lighting.*

J. Howard French Baltimore Pike Lima, Pa. 19060	*Bulbs for forcing.*
Janco Greenhouses Box 346 Beltsville, Md. 20705	*Greenhouse manufacturer and supplies.*
Jenkins Nursery P.O. Box 702 320 East 33rd Avenue Covington, La. 70433	*Bromeliads.*
John Scheepers, Inc. 63 Wall Street New York, N.Y. 10005	*Bulbs for forcing.*
Julius Roehrs Co. Route 33 Farmingdale, N.J. 07727	*Bromeliads, ferns, specimen and regular house plants.*
Kartuz Greenhouses 92 Chesnut Street Wilmington, Mass. 01887	*Begonias, gesneriads and other house plants.*
L. Easterbrook Greenhouses 10 Craig Street Butler, Ohio 44822	*Specimen and foliage plants.*
Lauray of Salisbury Undermountain Road, Rt. 41 Salisbury, Conn. 06068	*Gesneriads.*
Logee's Greenhouses Danielson, Conn. 06239	*Begonias, ferns, geraniums, herbs and other house plants.*
Lord & Burnham Irvington, N.Y. 10533	*Greenhouse manufacturers and supplies.*
McComb Greenhouses Route 1 New Straitsville, Ohio 43766	*Ferns, house plants.*

Merry Gardens Camden, Me. 04843	*Begonias, geraniums, ferns, herbs and other house plants.*
Mini-Roses Box 4355 Station A Dallas, Tex. 75208	*Miniature roses.*
Nor'East Miniature Roses 58 Hammond Street Rowley, Mass. 01969	*Miniature roses.*
Redwood Domes, C. Aptos, Calif. 95003	*Manufacturer of greenhouses.*
Rheinfrank & Assoc. 5414 Sierra Vista Ave. Los Angeles, Calif. 90038	*Fertilizers, soil mixes, greenhouse supplies, etc.*
Shoplite Co., Inc. 566 Franklin Avenue Nutley, N.J. 07110	*Artificial lighting supplies and fixtures.*
Three Springs Fisheries Lilypons, Md. 21717	*Water lilies and all other kinds of aquatic plants.*
Tube Craft, Inc. 1311 West 80th Street Cleveland, Ohio 44102	*Artificial lighting supplies and fixtures.*
Van Ness Water Gardens 2460 N. Euclid Avenue Upland, Calif. 91786	*Water lilies and all other kinds of aquatic plants.*
Verilux Inc. 35 Mason Street Greenwich, Conn. 06830	*TruBloom fluorescent lamps.*
Violets by Constantinov 3321 21st Street, Apt. 7 San Francisco, Calif. 94110	*Miniature and semi-miniature violets and gesneriads.*

W. Atlee Burpee Co. P.O. Box 6929 Philadelphia, Pa. 19132	*Seeds for house plants.*
Wildwood Gardens 14488 Rock Creek Road Chardon, Ohio 44024	*Bonsai plants and mosses.*
Wilson Brothers Roachdale, Ind. 46172	*Geraniums and other house plants.*
Yoshimura Bonsai Co., Inc. Spring Valley Road Ossining, N.Y. 10562	*Bonsai plants and supplies.*

THE SUMMING UP

How often have we heard, "It's not what we do but how we do it that counts"? Nowhere is it more applicable than in the decorative arts. Growing plants is a craft, demanding much skill; displaying them is an art. Certain principles and guidelines are essential to all forms of art, but after these have been mastered the rest is subject to our own particular taste, environment, background and that elusive ingredient known as flair. Here is where the fun lies and where our creative ability is fulfilled.

Making plants a part of our home is to bring them into our innermost sanctuary. As with furniture and accessories, the plants we select and the way we display them tell a great deal about our personalities and lifestyles. Because plants are alive and constantly changing, they bring an extra dimension to the home that furnishings can't. Excitement surrounds any living thing.

We take care when we select a frame for a painting or a base for a sculpture, and we give much thought to how we will group our paintings to show them off most effectively. The principle is the same with plants. They can have a major impact on our decorating schemes if we recognize their potential and take a little time and trouble to bring it out.

A certain amount of self-discipline is necessary. It is more effective to display six healthy plants, correctly potted in attractive, appropriate containers, than to have ten plants which are poorly groomed for lack of time and left to grow in their original ordinary pots for lack of interest. The wise interior gardener delays acquiring more plants until he can easily look after his existing collection. Quality wins over quantity in just about everything, and that includes decorating with plants.

BIBLIOGRAPHY

While this book is written primarily for the use of plants as part of the interior decoration of the home, it is my hope that the reader will develop a curiosity and a fondness for growing plants which will lead to a thirst for additional knowledge. The reader is bound to have a favorite among his plants: bromeliads or gesneriads or begonias or the wide world of ivies. Whatever his choice, specialized knowledge is needed and there are books to supply this. It's exciting to pass from the "beginner" stage to the "intermediate." All it takes is actual experience and reading as much as possible about the subject matter. A combination of both is essential, because horticulture is not a science—at least not as long as plants are living things subject to all the exceptions to the rules as are other living creatures. Your own experience may prove that what some "expert" tells you in a book ain't necessarily so! But these books in turn represent the accumulated experience of knowledgeable people, and we can benefit greatly by acquainting ourselves with them.

GENERAL BOOKS:

THE APARTMENT GARDENER, Florence and Stanley Dworkin, Signet. $1.50.

EXOTIC PLANT MANUAL, Alfred Byrd Graf, Scribner's. $37.50.

EXOTICA III, PICTORIAL CYCLOPEDIA OF EXOTIC PLANTS, Alfred Byrd Graf, Scribner's. $78.00.

FLOWERING HOUSE PLANTS, James U. Crockett, Time-Life. $7.95.

FOLIAGE HOUSE PLANTS, James U. Crockett, Time-Life. $7.95.

GARDEN IN YOUR HOUSE, Ernesta Drinker Ballard, Harper & Row. $8.95.

MAKING THINGS GROW, Thalassa Cruso, Knopf. $7.95.

THE POCKET ENCYCLOPEDIA OF INDOOR PLANTS IN COLOR, Age Nicolaisen, Macmillan. $5.95.

THE WORLD BOOK OF HOUSE PLANTS, Elvin McDonald, Popular Library. $1.25.

SPECIALIZED BOOKS:

BONSAI FOR AMERICANS, George F. Hull, Doubleday. $7.95.

BONSAI, TREES AND SHRUBS, Lynn R. Perry, Ronald. $8.50.

BROMELIADS, Victoria Padilla, Crown. $12.50.

BROOKLYN BOTANIC GARDEN HANDBOOKS. True gems of top information at prices everyone can afford. Some of the titles you might want to get: "Dwarfed Potted Trees—The Bonsai of Japan," "Handbook on Herbs," "Bulbs," "House Plants," "Greenhouse Handbook for the Amateur," "Succulents," "Bonsai: Special Techniques," "African Violets and Relatives," "Miniature Gardens," "Ferns," "Gardening under Artificial Light." Prices for the handbooks are from $1.25 to $2.50, from the Brooklyn Botanic Garden, 1000 Washington Avenue, Brooklyn, N.Y. 11225.

BULBS, James U. Crockett, Time-Life. $7.95.

CACTI AND SUCCULENTS, William C. Mulligan, Grosset & Dunlap. $1.95.

CACTI AS DECORATIVE PLANTS, Jack Kramer, Scribner's. $6.95.

DISEASES AND PESTS OF ORNAMENTAL PLANTS, P. P. Pirone, Ronald. $13.50.

FERNS AND PALMS FOR INTERIOR DECORATION, Jack Kramer, Scribner's. $6.95.

THE GARDENER'S BUG BOOK, Cynthia Westcott, Doubleday. $12.95.

GARDENING INDOORS UNDER LIGHTS, Frederick H. and Jacqueline L. Kranz, Viking. $7.95.

GARDENING UNDER GLASS, Jerome A. Eaton, Macmillan. $8.95.

GARDENING WITH HERBS, Helen Morgenthau Fox, Dover. $2.50.

GREENHOUSE GARDENING AS A HOBBY, James U. Crockett, Doubleday. $6.95.

GREENHOUSE GARDENING FOR FUN, Claire L. Blake, Morrow. $2.95.

THE INDOOR LIGHT GARDENING BOOK, George A. Elbert, Crown. $10.95.

THE INDOOR WATER GARDENER'S HOW-TO HANDBOOK, Peter Loewer, Walker. $5.95.

THE JAPANESE ART OF MINIATURE TREES AND LANDSCAPES, Yuji Yoshimura & G. M. Halford, Tuttle. $10.95.

HANGING GARDENS: BASKET PLANTS INDOORS AND OUT, Jack Kramer, Scribner's. $6.95.

HELEN VAN PELT WILSON'S AFRICAN VIOLET BOOK, Helen Van Pelt Wilson, Hawthorn. $7.95.

HERB GARDENING IN FIVE SEASONS, Adelma Grenier Simmons, Hawthorn. $7.95.

JOY OF GERANIUMS, Helen Van Pelt Wilson, Morrow. $4.45.

SUNSET BOOKS. Besides those from the Brooklyn Botanic Garden, this is my other favorite series of handbooks. These are handsomely illustrated. Send for: "Bonsai," "Gardening in Containers," "African Violets," "Bulbs," "Terrariums & Miniature Gardens," "Herbs," "House Plants," "Succulents and Cactus." Prices for the large soft-cover books are $1.95 each, available at garden supply centers or from Lane Magazine & Book Company, Menlo Park, Calif. 94025.

THE TERRARIUM BOOK, Charles M. Evans with Roberta Lee Pliner, Random House. $7.95.

INDEX